Doctors and Management in the National Health Service

D0413530

Health Services Management
Series Editors:
Chris Ham, Health Services Management Centre, University of Birmingham
Chris Heginbotham, The Riverside Mental Health Trust, London

The British National Health Service is one of the biggest and most complex organizations in the developed world. Employing around one million people and accounting for £36 billion of public expenditure, the Service is of major conern to both the public and politicians. Management within the NHS faces a series of challenges in ensuring that resources are deployed efficiently and effectively. These challenges include the planning and management of human resources, the integration of professionals into the management process, and making sure that services meet the needs of patients and the public.

Against this background, the Health Services Management series addresses the many issues and practical problems faced by people in managerial roles in health services.

Current and forthcoming titles

Justin Keen (ed.): *Information Management in Health Services*
John Øvretveit: *Purchasing for Health*
Richard Joss and Maurice Kogan: *Advancing Quality: Total Quality Management in the National Health Service*
Maurice Kogan and Sally Redfern *et al.*: *Making Use of Clinical Audit: A guide to practice in the health professions*
Judith Allsop and Linda Mulcahy: *Risk Management in Medical Settings*
Valerie Iles: *Really Managing Health Care*
Gordon Marnoch: *Doctors and Management in the National Health Service*
Steve Harrison: *Managing Health Services: A basic text*

Doctors and Management in the National Health Service

Gordon Marnoch

Open University Press
Buckingham · Philadelphia

Open University Press
Celtic Court
22 Ballmoor
Buckingham
MK18 1XW

and
1900 Frost Road, Suite 101
Bristol, PA 19007, USA

First Published 1996

A catalogue record of this book is available from the British Library

ISBN   0 335 19344 7 (pb)   0 335 19345 5 (hb)

Library of Congress Cataloging-in-Publication Data
Marnoch, Gordon, 1960–
    Doctors and management in the National Health Service / Gordon Marnoch.
        p. cm. — (Health services management)
    Includes bibliographical references and index.
    ISBN 0–335–19344–7 (pbk.). — ISBN 0–335–19345–5 (hb)
    1. National Health Service (Great Britain) 2. Physicians—Great Britain. 3. Health services administration—Great Britain.
I. Title. II. Series.
    [DNLM: 1. National Health Service (Great Britain) 2. State Medicine—organization & administration—Great Britain. 3. Health Care Reform—Great Britain. 4. Medical Directors—organization & administration—Great Britain. 1W 225 FA1M3d 1996]
RA395.G6M27 1996
362.1′0941—dc20
DNLM/DLC
for Library of Congress   96–19931
                                                                              CIP

Typeset by Graphicraft Typesetters Ltd, Hong Kong
Printed in Great Britain by St Edmundsbury Press, Bury St Edmunds, Suffolk

Contents

Acknowledgements

I would like to thank a number of people for the help or encouragement they offered to me during the course of writing this book. They include those close to me, in particular my partner Andrea Farrell, my mother Jean Marnoch and my daughter Kristina. At the University of Central Lancashire where the idea for a book was conceived, Ken Phillips who facilitated my study trip to the United States and who as a colleague on two research projects helped me develop ideas on managing doctors. At the University of Aberdeen, Lorna McKee, Angus Laing, John Reid, Nicola Dinnie, Rita Joshi, Ken Ross for listening to me air my thoughts, Bill Keogh and Graham Mowatt for their ideas on quality management, Grant Jordan and Frank Bealy for their ideas on centralization, Seonaidh Cotton for reading drafts of the manuscript and Caroline Rutherford for her administrative help in general. At the University of Southern Maine, Bruce Clary and Andy Coburn of the Muskie Institute. Chris Heginbotham for his useful advice as the series editor. All of the health professionals in Scotland, England and the United States whose willingness to share their experiences with me has been so important to this book. Finally, Joan Malherbe at Open University Press for putting up with my increasingly busy schedule during 1995. All the views expressed are, of course, my own.

1 Introduction: the management agenda for doctors

This book represents an attempt to come to terms with the impact of public services management reform on doctors working in the National Health Service (NHS) and examines the emergent possibilities for using doctors' skills in the management processes of the future. Three purposes are served by this introductory chapter. First, a discussion is conducted around the *management agenda* that doctors find themselves part of. At one level this involves identifying the ideological 'grip' that has dominated approaches to public services management in the United Kingdom over the past fifteen years. On a different level there is also a requirement to establish the context of doctors' engagement with the *act of management*. Secondly, there is a need to justify *management concepts* as tools to help in our understanding of the part played by doctors in delivering health services in the NHS and elsewhere. In relation to this task a brief discussion of *formula management* schemes is presented. Thirdly, the introductory chapter sets out the scheme of analysis contained in subsequent chapters.

The management agenda for doctors in the NHS

In establishing the background to the contemporary agenda for the NHS it is always worth pointing out the obvious fact that it has been almost exclusively politicians, rather than doctors' leaders in professional bodies, or in professional positions of leadership in hospitals, who have initiated the process of managerial reform in the NHS. The agenda for change has therefore been political rather than professional or clinical in character.

Jorgensen (1993: 229) has described the dynamics of administrative reform of the type familiar to NHS professionals as 'expressing the *spirit of the time*'. By this he means that the ideas and devices applied to public service organizations as diverse in function as the Inland Revenue service and the NHS were very similar – performance indicators, short-term contracts for managers, performance-related pay, decentralization, user-orientation, quality of service, contracting out, privatization and so on. It would be wrong, however, to assume that a revolution has taken place. Individual public service organizations have proved to be more and less susceptible to the spirit of the times. As a rough guide, those public service organizations that rely on professionals to deliver services, and where an element of flexible discretionary judgement is used to match skills to needs, have been more resistant than those employing white-collar staff in process tasks. Doctors are, in almost all respects, the most resistant of all professions to managerial encroachment. Yet exposure to the spirit of the times has deeply influenced the medical profession's stance in relation to management reform. Much 'discord' in the NHS followed from this exposure, to the extent that management as an activity became strongly associated with the 'monotonous litany' of 1980s managerialism, and latterly with free market ideology.

Public services generally were dominated by increasing attention to performance and output measurement during the 1980s. The NHS, however, was unusual in that the commitment of nominal leaders to the ideas of the moment did not guarantee the primacy of devices associated with managerialism at the operational levels of service delivery. Nor did the re-design of the nationalized health care system, along the market styled lines of the 1989 white paper *Working for Patients* readily incorporate the professionals within a new spirit of the times.

While the relationship between doctors and the health service management process has become increasingly strained since the late 1980s, it would be misleading to suggest that conflict is anything new in the NHS. The process whereby clinicians argued the case over claims for scarce resources with administrators was a traditional and important element in the management of the NHS prior to the reforms of the past decade. The issue is rather that the substance of conflict has changed. Administrators used to act as referees in the contest for resources. Doctors competed for the opportunity to develop the mix of health care provision in directions that they favoured. The system was such that administrators were content to exert only an indirect influence over strategic positions being adopted. Operational matters were quite definitely the preserve of the medical profession. Since the introduction of general management in the mid-1980s the programme to gain greater direct managerial control over operational and strategic matters in the NHS has progressed fitfully. Crucially, the conflict is increasingly taking place over the *process* of management rather than the *outputs* of management as understood in resource allocation terms. Conflict over who gets what is the lifeblood of healthy organizations; if there is no conflict it probably indicates apathy and lack of strategic vision. In contrast, conflicts over the part competing groups play in the management process is likely to divert energies away from actual decision making about strategic opportunities. In a commercial environment this sort of distraction may present an opportunity for competitors to take advantage. In the NHS it may lead to a situation where strategy is allowed to drift.

A puzzled relationship?

To outsiders it is perfectly logical to anticipate that the nationalized status of the NHS will imply a simple uniform relationship between doctors and their employers. This in turn could be expected to be a factor in clarifying the position existing between doctors and the management agenda, in comparison with, say the USA, where doctors are employed under numerous different arrangements. In reality this has not proved to be the case. It is relatively easy to establish that doctors working in hospitals are employed in contracts held with their employers in health authorities or NHS trusts and that the self-employed general practioners (GPs) are actually rewarded under a system that is enshrined in a lengthy 'contract' referred to as the 'Red Book'. Yet this does not entirely describe the relationship. In most other countries, including the USA and Germany, historically most doctors have enjoyed a self-employed status. In Britain, however, since 1948 the medical profession and individual doctors have been in a position that is best described as a unique form of public service. In the hospital and community care sectors they are salaried but frequently act as if they were self-employed paying little heed to the idea of line management. In the primary care sector, GPs are self-employed contractors to a single customer – the state.

The formal position between the state and the medical profession in the UK is a sum of parts that does not add up to either an administrative or commercial whole. In contrast the relationship between the self-employed office-based doctors, who are the core of the German health care system, and the state and insurers is highly proscribed. It is spelt out in legal-constitutional terms, where mutual rights, rules and obligations are enforced through obligatory membership of professional associations (Godt 1987: 460–4; Moran 1994: 49). The British relationship is the product of an *ad hoc* process of accommodations and concessions between the state and the medical profession. The relationship can be traced back to the imperial age where it was convenient for the state to offer the fledgling British Medical Association monopoly status in the regulation of medicine in the colonies. An aversion to providing a legal-constitutional identity for professional bodies and trade unions runs through British history (Phelps Brown 1983). 'Gentleman's agreements' were always preferred to constitutionally negotiated orders along the lines of the German model. In the USA a relationship between state and medical profession emerged out of commercial legal necessities which were a response to monopoly practices by insurers and providers.

Although receiving the bulk of their income from their employer, the nationalized NHS, doctors in hospital organizations, community care and in general practice have never perceived themselves as public servants operating under clearly stipulated codes of conduct, instructions and rules emanating from the parent ministry in London. Health care observers in the USA are often bewildered by the freedom accorded to publicly employed doctors in the NHS in relation to clinical matters when their own doctors, though usually self-employed, are enmeshed in a network of rules that constrain clinical choices. The absorption of a self-regulating culture into a nationalized health care system in 1948, gives the management change agenda a particular twist, unique to Britain.

As history reveals, doctors in the United Kingdom have consistently been against change – change of any kind for any reason – in the organizational arrangements for their employment in the NHS. This is unsurprising since, for the first forty years, any organizational change undertaken in the NHS avoided focusing on the medical profession. Consequently 'administrative tinkering' seemed an unnecessary distraction from the work of practising medicine. Post-Working for Patients doctors are, one way or another, participants in a process of change. The extent of their participation and the enthusiasm or resistance they bring to this process is clearly crucial to the delivery of health care in the United Kingdom. Adding to the uncertainty about the future relationship between the doctors and their responses to the management agenda are the 'local circumstances' of health service reform in Britain. The ghost of Thatcherism hangs over Working for Patients, making it difficult for many in the health services to delineate between crude public expenditure controls and genuine attempts at reforming the management process in the NHS.

The end of 'linear growth' and the inevitability of change

Until the mid-1980s, in both the US and the UK health care systems the medical profession practised in organizations that were underwritten by sustained growth in health care spending. The NHS enjoyed particularly rapid growth in the 1960s and 1970s just as the US health care system did on the back of the 'Great Society' health care reforms initiated by Lyndon Johnson during the same period (OECD 1987; Harrison *et al.* 1990: 38). In many respects the pressures currently facing doctors in the USA and the UK have similar origins and are rooted in the problem of finite resources meeting non-finite demands.

Historically, the practice of medicine has been regulated not managed, although this situation is unlikely to continue. The form that regulation has taken in different health care systems varies at the margins but with one common feature – doctors regulate doctors. In Britain, as in the USA and the EU countries, doctors will continue to regulate doctors in respect of clinical practice but this form of control is likely to be supplemented with behaviour management. How balances between older forms of regulation and newer forms of resource-orientated managed care are achieved is not yet clear. In state funded systems the tendency has been to rely on global expenditure capping, whereas in demand driven health care systems, such as those of France and the USA, there is relatively little government power in respect of exercising 'remote control' over resources consumed by health care. In the USA in particular the route to capping health care expenditure is taking a markedly different form from that employed in the UK and is reliant on altering individual clinician's behaviour.

Whatever the political-financial basis of the health care system the participation of doctors in the process of discovering innovative organizational methods for delivering new services efficiently and effectively is essential. Without participation and behavioural change on the part of doctors government will continue to rely on budget ceilings as the primary means of regulating health care activity. As Thompson argues this can impose constraints on the evolutionary structure of the health care system in response to technical, scientific and management breakthroughs (Thompson 1992).

If Working for Patients represented the high point of the Thatcherite paradigm as applied to the NHS, then perhaps another 'spirit of the times' is emerging around the type of *new public management* articulated by the US authors Osborne and Gaebler (1992) in *Reinventing Government*. Ideas expressed in this influential book are highly regarded by those politicians who now occupy the centre field in US and UK politics. The basic wound-healing message is that there is no dichotomy between private and public solutions to social problems. Problems cannot be left to the marketplace any more than they can be 'solved' by the act of state intervention. Instead the state must be prepared to use the full range of available techniques and instruments to pursue the act of governance. Supporters of the new public management believe in entrepreneurial government which is about setting policies, delivering funds to action-orientated organizations and evaluating impacts. Such practices are in sharp contrast to the previous fashion of expanding the operational activities of government. Government, it is argued, should not be in the business of delivering services itself but instead contract with semi-independent or independent provider agencies. Osborne and Gaebler dubbed this as 'steering versus rowing'. Adopting such a role is how government can achieve 'more bang out of every buck'. The most profitable management techniques, they argue, are to be found in participatory organizations. New public management therefore implicitly challenges the traditional practices of NHS management in the sense that it can only be activated if the participation of the medical profession is forthcoming. It must be remembered in this context that doctors have control over core operational processes. Only doctors have the credibility to assess benefits to patients, measure benefits and carry out the evaluation that informs the new public management. Reinvented government and its health care provider agencies therefore require active participation in the management process by doctors, whether in the context of the market driven USA or the nationalized NHS.

In spite of the adversarial stances adopted by the state and the medical profession over the last decade in the UK there has been no winner. Confident self-assertion in relation to management reform might have been expected of the medical profession, but instead the politics of the Thatcher era produced a highly defensive stance. Some observers of the UK health service system may conclude that doctors have succeeded in slowing down ill-conceived reforms (Health Service Journal/Glaxo Healthy Debate 1993). Such a view unfortunately ignores the significance of a series of developments in medical practice which have come of age in clinical terms: minimally invasive techniques, day surgery, community hospitals and polyclinics (Hunter 1993).

In contrast to the USA where the people are said to distrust politics and instinctively reach for market solutions, the British public appear to mistrust markets *and* politics when it comes to health care. Perhaps during an era of suspicion over the activities of government, the time is ripe for the medical profession to take the lead in organizational reform. A conceit exists in central government as to the importance of the reforms they have pursued over the past ten years. The focus of this book will therefore not be centred on legislation and Management Executive directives, but instead will focus on the activity of management in the NHS as it engages with doctors – the key profession in any advanced system of health care. As the nature of health care is changes, the practices and philosophies associated with the shift from hospital to community care may ultimately prove of more lasting consequence than all of the performance indicator, league table driven managerialism that so alienated the health service professions in the last ten years.

Doctors and management

Doctors have an ambivalent relationship to the management process in the NHS. This is due partly to a lack of agreement over what management actually is. A management researcher who recently conducted extensive research with the staff of a large telecommunications manufacturer concluded that there are three senses in which we use the word 'management' (Watson 1994: 34–5):

1 Management as function: as the *overall steering* or *directing* of an organization.
2 Management as activities: as a set of *activities* carried out in order to bring about the overall steering or directing of the organization.
3 Management as a team of people: as the *group of people* responsible for steering or directing the organization through carrying out the various activities which make this possible.

It is legitimate to query, as Watson does, what we mean when, as individuals and groups of professionals, we conclude that the 'management is no good around here'? In certain instances we mean the top management do not understand the organization. In other cases we are bemoaning the ineffectiveness of activities being carried out by subordinates. Culpability may here lie with the designers of the organizational process. Occasionally we may even recognize our own failings as members of a management team. The medical profession needs to engage with all three aspects of the management process.

The leadership gap

> The new order is a society of organisations, they rule over and above or in spite of political rule because they are in charge of central function of making knowledge productive.
>
> (Drucker 1992)

Drucker has identified a key development in western society. Coincident with the increased dependency on a knowledge-based economy there seems to be a decline in the public's faith in the political system to produce solutions to social and economic problems. As a trend, this is most evident in the USA but is clearly influencing British society as well. As people develop a more critical appreciation of public services it seems clear that the National Health Service has an increasingly important part to play in governance – balancing the competing claims of society's stakeholders.

As political parties have attracted increasing scorn or sheer indifference, the NHS enjoys an exulted position in British society. The public nature of the NHS and its heavy dependency on the role played by the medical profession make it both a potentially strong organization for governance and also a particularly vulnerable one if more active participation in the management process is not sought by the medical profession at every level. The role played by professionals in the management of the NHS is an issue that has consequences beyond that of health care.

Thinking about management

Given the experience of the managerialist 1980s and the market 1990s, doctors are rightly sceptical regarding the efficacy of management thinking in relation to the delivery of health services. Pascale has identified the sheer variety of 'faddy' managerial 'fixes' proffered by the gurus in the last twenty years. He describes the list as a 'Who's Who' of business hype – 'Theory Z, Matrix, managerial grid, T-Groups, entrepreneurship, Demassing and One Minute Managing.' These are 'hot ideas' which form the products sold by the less reputable management consultants. It has been pointed out that they have a shelf life in the business world roughly equivalent to a supermarket lettuce in some cases. Pascale (1990: 18–22) quotes the marketing manager of a large American equipment manufacturer:

> In the past eighteen months, we have heard that profit is more important than revenue, quality is more important than profit, that people

are more important than profit, that customers are more important than our people, that big customers are more important than our small customers, and that growth is the key to our success. No wonder our performance is inconsistent.

Pascale notes that the great 'quality circles' discovered by American corporations in the early 1980s had been largely discontinued by 1986. Pascale believes that while generic management techniques may have some intrinsic value, it is commitment and sustainability that are the real factors in measuring impact rather than a simple question of success or failure when a technique is introduced. 'Mindsets' can dominate organizations. According to the former boss of ICI, Sir John Harvey Jones (1993: 1–12), the 1960s were the decade of counting everything, which meant it was also the decade of the accountant, 'if you can't measure it don't manage it'. By the 1970s the penny began to drop that counting everything and refining accounting systems did not actually seem to achieve that much. Figures could only help scale managers' ideas – they can not be a substitute for subjective judgement. Much effort was spent verifying the accuracy of data rather than using it. Planning was fashionable and seen as the way forward for industry and government. But five-year forecasts that assumed no surprises proved to be dangerous. Harvey Jones believes that the Japanese have only ever used information as a means of calibrating subjective judgements and have not attempted to take the judgement out of management.

Until the 1980s the public services in the UK remained largely immune to the lure of formula management techniques and management mindsets. Over the course of the last decade, however, public service managers, like their colleagues in the private sector, have increasingly clutched at the latest fix-all technique. Doctors, on the other hand, in the author's experience, preferred to be ignorant of the latest fad. If they were aware of the latest management trick they remained bemused by the whole business.

Pascale, like Harvey Jones and Peters (1993), is interested in interpreting the 'ideological undertow' that carries an organization forward, rather than any management trick. These writers have been able to contextualize patterns of managerial behaviour and identify the emergence of a new spirit of the times that is often hard to discern from a practitioner perspective. Not unsurprisingly, the tendency has been for management thinkers to pay increasing attention to the practices employed by the great Japanese corporations whose impact on the world economy became dominant in the 1990s.

Matsushista, leader of one of the biggest electronics firms in Japan, has said:

> business, we know, is now so complex and difficult, the survival of firms so hazardous in an environment increasingly unpredictable, competitive and fraught with danger, that their continued existence depends on the day-to-day mobilisation of every ounce of intelligence.
>
> (Pascale 1990: 27)

In other words the simple seemingly self-evident assumption that managers do the thinking while the workers wield the screwdrivers has been replaced with a 'mindset' that sees workers as intellectual as much as physical assets. Harsh facts mean that management now takes place on a totally different terrain and global environment. In his current role as management sage Harvey Jones reasons that the sacred cows of management have gone. The 'biggest will always win', 'establish economies of scale in production and marketing' – these principles are now seen as sources of inflexibility. Tom Peters, the American management guru, has also added to the new consensus that 'big' is no longer viable. While it is questionable whether the size of an organization is the critical factor in success, evidence suggests that the ability to respond quickly to market opportunities has become crucial.

Harvey Jones points out that in manufacturing today, labour costs are never usually more than 20 per cent. In fully robotized plants, labour costs are less than 10 per cent and falling. There is therefore not much advantage in cutting labour costs from 7 to 6 per cent. Production is rapidly becoming a fixed cost. The Sonys and Hondas are successful because they excel in research and development, advertising, quality control, distribution and accounting. Functions that were formerly overheads are now the central costs and the key variables for success or failure in the business. This implies a more substantial dependency on knowledge.

The NHS employs approximately 100,000 doctors – 20,000 specialists in the secondary sector, 33,000 GPs, 40,000 in training grades and 7000 in public health (Office of Health Economics 1995). Given the current condition of NHS management it is inevitable that there are many expensive, highly educated people whose talents are not being utilized in the management process. The message to be drawn from the writers on management is that the successful organizations of the 1990s will be those who succeed in empowering employees at every grade enabling them to contribute to the general management process at strategic and operational levels. The strategic managers at the peak level will have to realize their new dependency on the expertise of those at the operational end. Harvey Jones, Pascale and Peters call it managing 'on the run', 'maintaining a state of constructive equilibrium' and 'managing chaos'. The age of managing by uniformity and standardization is apparently over. Health care may be subjected to the same type of groundshifting changes.

The scheme of analysis

Subsequent chapters attempt to examine what *has* happened to the relationship between doctors and the management process in the NHS and, on the basis of evidence available, speculate on how the connection between medical knowledge and organizational change can in practice be developed.

In Chapter 2 a brief account of the history of medical management is presented. A feature of this chapter is the distinction made between reform at the political or structural level, administrator-led implementation in the health service localities, and the separateness of organizational changes implemented by doctors. The lack of articulation between the management process as experienced by doctors and that controlled by non-professionals at structural and administrative levels is discussed. A chronology is provided in the form of a table based on the categories used above. Chapter 2 also draws attention to the tightening of the hierarchical management change between 1984 and 1989 after the introduction of the Griffiths Report (National Health Service Management Inquiry 1983).

In Chapter 3 the impact of the 'management by crisis' circumstances brought in by the implementation of Working for Patients is reviewed from the perspective of medical management. The part played by doctors in managing the internal market is critically examined. Particular attention is paid to the impact that the new internal market requirements and relationships are making on the capacity of GPs to manage for innovation. The need for the NHS trusts to reconsider the relationship between clinicians and the management process is also examined. The utility of medical management techniques emphasized in the 1989 White Paper are briefly considered. Chapter 3 concludes with the argument that the dynamic qualities of the internal market are largely illusory. Misunderstandings concerning the relationship of professional relationships, ill-designed financial management systems and political fright have all reduced the consequent impact of the environmental turbulence formulated in Working for Patients.

Chapter 4 is concerned with the new medical managers in NHS trusts. The roles of medical directors and clinical directors are critically examined. Differing expectations being made of medical directors and clinical directors in individual trusts is an emerging feature of the NHS. The limitations and potentials of the new medical managers are discussed.

Chapter 5 is concerned with the impact of performance management in relation to doctors. The politics of performance management are established, with the prospects of an evaluation-led NHS examined. Problems surrounding the competing claims of stakeholders and the different structures of thought in relation to health care are discussed and represented in an illustrative table. A framework for understanding specific performance management technologies is developed through the separation of 'externally owned and driven' schemes from medical profession 'owned and driven' initiatives. Comparison is made with the development of management-orientated technologies for clinical control in the US health care system. Taking TQM (total quality management) as an example, an assessment is made of the likely impact of 'off the peg management systems' in the context of the NHS. Finally, the potential shock-wave that state sponsored 'consumerism' can provide is considered. A map is used to summarize, from a doctor's perspective, the different characteristics of performance management schemes discussed in Chapter 5 according to ownership and the degree of control implied.

Chapter 6 examines issues of organizational design in relation to the management of doctors. Mintzberg's standard classifications of organizational design, principally the 'machine organization', the 'professional organization' and the 'innovative organization' are compared with organizational structures constructed around the concept of the 'network organization'. The viability of competing organizational design in the context of the NHS is considered, with the implications for doctors being kept in particular focus. A table is provided to summarize the different strengths and weaknesses of organizational types examined.

Chapter 7 serves as a conclusion but also brings in a comparative element to the analysis of the relationship between doctors and management in the NHS. Reactions of the medical profession in the US to the growth of 'managed care' are examined as a means of drawing attention to the relative organizational conservatism of doctors in the NHS. An attempt is made to explore the lessons that can be taken from the management of doctors in US health maintenance organizations. The case for a much enhanced role in the governance of health care in the UK is made.

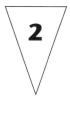

2 The pre-history of contemporary medical management in the National Health Service

The history of the relationship of doctors to the management process in the NHS is characterized by a lack of articulation between strategic or political levels and operational activities dominated by the profession. In this chapter the aim is to provide a concise description of the development of what is in conventional organizational terms an unusual relationship. A chronology of major events in the development of the NHS is used to demonstrate the failure to connect policy and structural reform to the world of the medical profession. Establishing such a pre-history of the internal market medical management relationships of the 1990s is neccessary in order to place recent changes in perspective.

Doctors have, it should be stressed, always played key roles in the management process used to deliver health care within the NHS. At government or strategic level doctors have been involved since the inception of the NHS in the business of reconciling activity levels with available resources. They have always given advice on the formulae used to share out resources on a regional and service basis (Ham 1992: 177–80). Medical leaders have also been instrumental in constructing concepts of the population's health needs. Patterns of service delivery and the growth of new sub-specialties and treatments have been largely shaped by the profession. The General Medical Council (GMC), Royal Colleges and universities have primary responsibility for ensuring medical standards are set and met in medical training. At the level of hospital units and individual departments, senior doctors have been responsible for establishing professional standards of work. The same senior professionals were also expected to take part in an allocation process whereby they pursued the claims of their specialist colleagues for increased resources. At the level of the individual doctor practising in the secondary care sector an assumption has implicitly existed that they maximize the effectiveness of their own work within the given hospital context. Clearly, a major contribution to the organizational life of a hospital is made by doctors at the point of service delivery where their special knowledge base gives them full responsibility for patient care management. In general practice, doctors have a responsibility for delivering their contractual responsibilities to the NHS and running a small business that employs support staff. (The management allowance to fundholding practices is £35,000 per annum.)

It may be claimed that doctors are, as a profession, fulfilling the roles typically expected of managers already. Doctors are involved in all the key roles identified in classical management writings:

1 *Management is about forecasting the future.* Doctors are central to forecasting at central and local levels. A specialist branch of the profession – public health – is devoted to this task.
2 *Managers are organizers.* They structure human and physical aspects of the organization. Doctors have been instrumental in establishing patterns of organization in hospitals and local medical centres and in relationships between primary and secondary sectors.
3 *Managers are commanders.* They need the authority to issue orders. Consultants are most obviously commanders within the clinical team or firm they head up. GPs are commanders leading a small business.
4 *Management is about coordination* – overseeing the work of others. Professional bodies are there to coordinate the provision of medical personnel. At local level doctors coordinate colleagues and the use of a range of human resources, supplies and technical equipment.
5 *Managers are controllers*, ensuring that everything occurs in conformity with established rule and expressed command. Once again the Royal Colleges have a key role while the work of enforcing standards is an important role taken by doctors as individuals and in relation to peers at the local level. (Wilson and Rosenfeld 1990: 299)

A more recent description of the work of the manager, based on empirical observation rather than idealization, emphasizes less grand management tasks, such as fire fighting and building consensus, and the roles involved in rituals, linking, intuition, figure head, information (Stewart 1967; Mintzberg 1973). No matter which description is preferred the contribution being made by doctors to these tasks typically has not been seen as management in the past. Rather it has been conceived in professional terms as something which is medical in nature and not to be addressed in managerial terms. Certainly the language used to describe the type of role played by doctors in these areas was clinical and not derived from the standard vocabulary of organizational life.

Partial involvement of doctors in the management process

While acknowledging the contribution made at a strategic resource allocation level it can also be claimed that the major contribution made by doctors has been at the point of delivery, where their special knowledge base accords them full responsibility for patient care management. Doctors have typically conceived this role in professional as opposed to management terms in the sense that patients' needs have been paramount in decisions they make. The concept of medical autonomy has often been used to explain the difference between professional and managerial judgement. Doctors as professionals reserve the right to decide who to treat, when to treat them and how to treat them. Of course, clinical judgement takes place in the real world of organizational constraints, where resources are finite. In the regulation of resource use, informal understandings concerning the setting of the parameters of choice has to be made within a given organizational context. Here senior clinicians have a major responsibility for securing a position of accommodation for their colleagues within the resource circumstance prevailing at the time.

While doctors were visibly involved in aspects of the management process, this traditional medical input did not add up to a coherent role in the management process. The medical professions' contribution to the management process in the NHS has historically been patchy and lacking in codification. The contribution made at a strategic resource allocation level is twofold. The major input here tends typically to be conceived in political terms, deriving as it does from either the state sanctioned monopoly over medical representation and accreditation under the Medical Act of 1858 which established General Medical Council (GMC) and Royal Colleges as the licensed regulatory bodies, or from the British Medical Association's (BMA) equally exclusive rights as the doctors' negotiating body (Stacey 1992: 15–26; Moran and Wood 1993: 35–8). In a people dominated organization like the NHS the regulatory and bargaining roles played by the GMC and BMA over such issues as training specialists, medical pay and manpower take on substantial significance. Yet when the BMA's senior professional representatives bargain with departmental ministers and officials, or the Royal Colleges or GMC act to regulate aspects of professional life, this is seen as a medical rather than managerial activity, albeit a medical role demanding political skills (Harrison *et al.* 1992: 22–3).

On a less political level there is also the input made to the doctors belonging to the public health specialism. The public health function dates back to the Poor Laws of 1834 when parishes were required to appoint medical officers. Over time the role of the public health doctor has become associated with the administration and planning of patterns of medical service provision in localities. That chief medical officers have played a significant role in the management of health boards is not in question, although their precise contributions tended to vary considerably. In some localities the role was dominated by the post-holder's interest in epidemiology and consequent planning issues, while in others the role would tend towards acting as an intermediary between the profession and the health authority's administrators. In recent years the role of public health doctors has become further confused, with 'technical' aspects of the job, such as the interpretation of health care data and the clarification of health service responsibilities to populations served, becoming more important than the administrative role previously fulfilled by specialists in this field. At central government level in England and Scotland the Chief Medical Officer remains an important figure providing the link between politicians and the profession.

While recognizing the major contribution made by doctors to the management process in the NHS, the conclusion must be drawn that there has been little organizational basis to articulate the different levels of involvement. Sir Roy Griffith's claim that doctors were natural managers has a ring of truth about it, but it should also be noted that the sum total of their efforts was historically uneven and not designed according to any recognizable organizational plan (National Health Service Management Inquiry 1983). In short, there is no medical management *system* in the NHS. There has been no systematic appraisal of the role of doctors in the management processes of the NHS. Reform that has taken place in the area of medical management has been tangential to mainstream administrative reform.

Table 2.1 sets out major management changes in the NHS from 1948 to the present day. The reforms are presented under three classifications highlighting the disjuncture that exists between levels of management action in the NHS. Column one records management reforms that took place on a structural level, being based on strategic decisions taken by politicians, Department of Health officials and senior medical representatives. The principle instruments of implementation being Acts of Parliament and action on ministerial inquiries. In organizational terms, this is the strategic level. Column two lists changes that, while initiated at the level of policy, have been enacted under the direction of locally based NHS administrators, medical and nursing representatives and lay members of boards of administration. This is the implementational control level. The third column lists developments which can clearly be seen to centrally involve doctors – the operational level.

The first phase: the slack chain, 1948–76

The NHS is, on the face of it, a typical government bureaucracy with a Department headed by a Secretary of State at its apex. However, this simple representation is only partly accurate. A bureaucracy does exist in the NHS but it fails to straddle all three levels of management. The centre can issue edicts which will be taken up and implemented at the localities level but only in so far as it involves actions carried out by professional administrators (now always described as managers), rather than the key operational staff – the doctors. Table 2.1 shows that the NHS Act of 1946 was implemented by Ministry of Health civil servants who delegated to staff based in the localities, where in turn an administrative structure was created. This structure involved Regional Hospital Boards and Hospital

Table 2.1 The history of structural, management and clinician led change 1948–96

Structural changes	Management changes	Changes considered/implemented by clinicians
Departmental implemented 1948 – Ministry of Health at peak of structure based on 19 regions delegating to a locally based tripartite structure controlling hospitals, primary care and local authority run public health programmes	Regional Hospital Boards established delegated operational management to Hospital Management Committees or Boards of Governors in Scotland. Teaching hospitals reported directly to Ministry of Health. Role of chief administrator created at Committee/Board level. Responsibilities shared with Matron and Medical Superintendent at hospital level	Consultants accept employment by Regional Health Board or Board of Governors of teaching hospital GPs employed as private contractors
	1956 – Bradbeer Committee endorses triumvirate style of management	
1962 – Hospital Plan for England and Wales created District General Hospital		1962 – Porritt Committee reports for BMA advising that tripartite structure be replaced with a unified authority using doctors to administer the three functions created in 1948
	1966 – Farquarson-Lang advocates replacement of triumvirate model with chief executive	1966 – Advisory Committee (Ministry of Health) recommends clearer definition of consultants' responsibilities and more peer review

Table 2.1 (continued)

Structural changes	Management changes	Changes considered/ implemented by clinicians
		1967 – Cogwheel Reports (Ministry and profession) recommend specialty division structure as basis for medical representation on Medical Executive Committee
1974 – tripartite structure replaced with area health authorities in England and area health boards in Scotland, assuming line responsibility for all hospital services	1972 – Grey Book (DHSS and NHS) recommends strengthening of consensus decision making	
1978 – RAWP – structural change to resource allocation		
1982 – areas replaced with district structure in England similar change in Scotland, both cases to bring in degree of coterminancy with local authority boundaries		1982 – Management Budgeting/Resource Management experiments begin
	1984 – implementation of general management at region, district and hospital levels. End of consensus management. Introduction of performance-related pay for management class. Increase in 'tautness' of chain of command between tiers. Greater attention to performance indicators. Extension of the Management budgeting/ resource management initiative	1987 – Guy's experiment with Johns Hopkins clinical directorate model

Table 2.1 (continued)

Structural changes	Management changes	Changes considered/implemented by clinicians
1990 – NHS and Community Care Act: internal market; NHS Trusts; GP fundholders	Purchaser-provider roles established on basis of self-governing NHS Trusts who sell services to health authorities and a new type of fundholding general practice	1990 – Clinical directorates established in Trusts. Medical representatives appointed Trust boards. Medical audit given greater formal importance in both secondary and primary care sectors
	Boards of health authorities reduced in size and contain higher proportion of people from 'business community' authority control to Trust status	1990 – new contract for general practice, increases importance of immunization and screening service provided by GPs
	1992–95 – Merger activity undertaken on a voluntary basis	GP fundholding begins – 11,000 out of 33,000 GPs now in fundholding practices covering 40% population, buying about 30% of their lists health care needs, 5700 GPs are members of National Association of Commissioning GPs (advise DHAs on purchasing) 102 groups covering 11 million patients
1994 – ME outposts in England. Number of regions reduced to 6		
1994 – Banks Report 1994 – Bottomley review	1994 – virtual completion of hospital and community care units re-designation as trusts	1994 – extension of GP fundholding
1996 – DHAs and FHSAs due to be merged in England		1995 – Revised arrangements for consultants distinction awards

Management Committees typically managing a group of hospitals. Chief administrative officers were appointed to take charge at these levels. Control at the level of the hospital was placed in the hands of a triumvirate: hospital secretary (administrator), medical administrator and matron. Local authorities remained responsible for a range of public health functions and ambulance services. Following the practice established in local government, a health committee took responsibility for policy matters while a doctor was appointed to the post of Medical Officer of Health. GPs became contracted to locally based Executive Councils. These bodies were also responsible for the contracting of other primary health care providers including dentists, pharmacists and opticians (Ham 1992: 15–18). Before the formation of the NHS, GPs had worked mainly as single-handed professionals (Marinker 1987). After 1948, GPs began to see the benefits of working in partnerships. Soutter *et al.* (1995) claim the benefits were clear: a young doctor would have difficulty finding sufficient capital to buy suitable premises while a senior doctor would wish to protect his investment in the practice premises. A partner also meant a lesser workload as far as 24-hour cover was concerned. The partnerships formed after 1948 were both business-centred and practice-centred. The organization formed had both financial and professional objectives to fulfil.

The changes for the medical profession were certainly significant in the sense that its members became either employees or contractors to the new NHS and were thus expected to serve the population as a whole. In spite of its magnitude as a political reform the strategically based structural design and implementational apparatuses involved in the creation of the NHS did not cause a massive change at the operational level of clinical practice. Hospital doctors remained largely free from managerial control in the normal sense implied by employment in a supposedly unified organization. Practices and customs pertaining to day-to-day patient management were left in isolation from the new administrative apparatuses. The structure created in 1948 could conceivably be regarded as an administrative facade put there to disguise the lack of change at the operational level. Consequently, the inclination and ability of the central strategic level to initiate and manage change has remained a central flaw in the organization. Perhaps it is even the case that more significant changes at operational level were to be found in the deepening divide between the secondary and primary based professionals.

As spiralling costs focused attention on the financial basis for the NHS, inevitably the lack of a true management system became apparent to the politicians and administrators nominally in charge of the service and to the medical profession itself. Harrison (1994: 11–16) has recorded the sharpening focus on management issues which was signified in the Guillebaud Committee's call for more 'oversight and supervision', the Bradbeer Report's affirmation of the triumvirate arrangement at hospital level and the continued stewardship of chief administrators at group level. Six years later, the BMA-sponsored Porritt Committee called for the integration of the tripartite structure, but with a doctor being appointed to take administrative responsibility for the three functions.

The unease over the management of hospitals continued with a Ministry advisory committee contrasting the lack of clarity over the management roles of hospital consultants when comparisons were attempted with 'industrial managers'. In the same year the controversial Farquarson-Lang Report called for the appointment of chief executives with clear leadership responsibility at regional and local levels in Scotland. Farquarson-Lang refuted the Porritt Committee's argument for appointing medically qualified administrators to these posts (Scottish Health Services Council 1966).

Acting positively in respect of management of the NHS proved politically unattractive and successive governments were keener to make adjustments to the administrative facade rather than construct something solid behind it in terms of management and organization. The specific question of doctors and their relationship to the management process was resolved through the device of a joint Ministry-General Medical Council committee which produced the 'Cogwheel Reports'. The document was presented in a cover that graphically depicted specialist interdependency in the form of meshing cogwheels. The metaphor overstated the organizational exactitude of the recommendations which were no more than an exhortation for the medical staff to organize along the lines of a basic model already in existence in many hospitals. Hospital-based medical specialties were encouraged to organize into 'divisions' which would in turn send a delegate to a Medical Executive Committee. This committee would in effect represent the medical constituency within the hospital or group of hospitals it served. Its chairman would be the medical profession's symbolic figurehead, but with no properly defined powers or organizational responsibilities. This was a political rather than a managerial system for ensuring medical interests were constituted in a broadly coherent pattern throughout Britain (Ministry of Health 1967). Implementation of the Cogwheel recommendations was haphazard and, more importantly, was a development which headed off, rather than confronted, the old problem of a lack of articulation between strategic, locality and operational management in the NHS. The medical profession remained adrift of managerial control from the higher levels in the NHS organization.

The 1974 re-organization which was mainly concerned to match the NHS structure to the recently reorganized local authorities also endorsed the relationship between administrators and the medical profession. The lack of articulation between medical and administrative actions was thus formally recognized. A tendency to avert attention from the missing management-medical connections in NHS management was turned into a virtue. Similarly, the concept of the NHS as a political organization, where the professional constituencies came together in a decision-making forum was thus firmed up. The so-called Grey Book on health service management recorded the deliberations of a ministerial inquiry confirming the government's faith in what was now referred to as consensus decision making.

The political nature of consensus decision making has been written about in some depth elsewhere (Harrison 1988: 9–29). The 1972 White Paper, which the Conservatives produced and which formed the basis for the 1974 reorganization, states the position in fairly clear terms:

> The organisational changes will not affect the professional relationship between individual patients and individual professional workers on which the complex of health services is so largely based. The professional workers will retain their clinical freedom – governed as it is by the bounds of professional knowledge and ethics and the resources that are available – to do as they think best for the patients.
>
> (DHSS, 1972, vii)

Given the first sentence, sceptics assessing the worth of the 1974 reorganization, which replaced the old tripartite structure involving local authorities with a new geographically based hierarchy of regions and areas, might have queried 'why bother then?'. The government returned to the question of geographical coverage again in 1982, this time replacing the areas with a larger number of districts. This amounted to manageable change which could be implemented without the operational co-operation of the medical profession.

The second phase: tightening the chain, 1976–90

From the mid-1970s central government began to impose 'cash limits' on the regional and district levels of the NHS. This proved a significant moment in the history of the NHS. From 1976 onwards the then Labour government pursued a new approach to controlling public spending – the resource allocation process had been reversed. Previously, governments had underwritten the funding for a particular agreed volume of health service provision. This meant that even if inflation in the proceeding year boosted the actual cash cost of providing the agreed level of service the government would still meet its commitment. The system worked in inflation proofed 'funny money' (Thain 1985; Thain and Wright 1989: 149–62). With the sobering experience of negotiating with the International Monetary Fund for a loan behind them, the Labour government now only agreed to provide a cash sum to the NHS. (The system was applied more or less uniformly across the whole area of government expenditure.) Management in the localities had to accept a cash figure at the outset of a financial year and try to keep expenditure within that limit. The days of government making good shortfalls caused by inflation or some other reason such as a higher than expected round of wage increases were over. This greatly increased the taughtness of the managerial chain between central and locality levels. The NHS had entered a new phase in its development in which centralized management control increasingly made its influence felt.

In spite of the financial 'straightening' going on between the Treasury and the spending departments (like the Department of Health) the conviction to draw together the structural, locality and operational levels in a fully articulated system for controlling the NHS had not yet emerged. The Resource Allocation Working Party (RAWP) programme launched in 1978 was a bid to re-allocate resources away from the 'over-provisioned' areas, such as the south east of England, to historically 'under-funded' localities (Jones and Prowle 1984). While government was now embarking on the long road towards greater centralized financial control over public services, RAWP was still premised on an arm's length philosophy of management control. A resource initiative like RAWP could be centrally controlled and while it indirectly impinged on doctors' actions the programme could still be launched at considerable distance from the operational level.

It was reasonably well acknowledged in the early 1980s that the NHS accounting systems, while now generating patient costs by institution or department, did not serve as a mechanism for controlling clinical resources – that is, the medical staff, nursing staff, pharmaceuticals, medical supplies, theatre time, beds – used in patient care. In the area of financial control perhaps more than any other aspect of management there was still a lack of connection with the work carried out by doctors. The doctors made little input to the accounting system in the 1970s and conversely were little influenced by financial controls on a day-to-day basis (though they had to ultimately live within global resource constraints). Heads of functional departments such as pathology, nursing or pharmacy, had little influence over the usage made by doctors of the resource they provided (Pollitt *et al.* 1988: 213–34). At worst, control over the resource consuming implications of clinical activity took the form of closing down a sub-specialty ward or clinic for a few weeks. Clearly, the lack of a system for controlling clinical resource use was a major organizational weakness. It is difficult to see a parallel situation being allowed to persist in any commercial organization.

Experiments with budgeting systems designed to link management to clinical activity were begun under the auspices of the CASPE research unit in three health authorities during the early 1980s. Doctors were given responsibility to keep within an overall budget and allowed to move expenditure from one sub-budget heading to another (known as 'virement'). Clinical budgeting might have remained a theoretically 'interesting' project destined never to be acted upon but for the circumstances developing at the strategic political level of the NHS. An electoral commitment to cut public expenditure began to be translated into a set of managerialist interventions in the NHS. The Department of Health began developing performance indicators. In September 1983, some 70 metrics relating to clinical work, finance, manpower, support services and estate management were established from already available data. The clinical indicators related mainly to the use of clinical facilities within broad specialty groups and included efficiency measures such as average length of hospital stay, throughput of patients per bed per annum, turnover interval between cases occupying a bed, and the ratio of return outpatient visits to new outpatients. Within two months later, the Secretary of State Norman Fowler announced a further two initiatives formulated in the same managerialist spirit. A national enquiry was established to identify underused and surplus land and property with a view to discovering how it could be disposed of if possible. In August 1983, a review of NHS Audit arrangements was announced which resulted in a greater political emphasis on 'value for money'. Then in October, Norman Fowler announced to the Conservative Party conference that a manpower review was to take place. He was responding at least in part to the perennial political clamour against a supposed surplus of unproductive managers in the NHS. He decided to form a small team, headed by people from private industry, who would report quickly on the issues in hand (Harrison *et al.* 1992: 41–4).

Immediately afterwards, an announcement was made that a firm of chartered accountants was to study the possibility of cash-limiting Family Practitioner Committee budgets. These committees were the funding bodies for primary care in England. In January 1983, central control of NHS manpower numbers was raised as a matter of immediate concern and in February came news that the government was considering restrictions on doctors' rights to prescribe freely. In November, the government went part of the way towards deciding on this question when it curtailed the use of a range of expensive 'branded' drugs, meaning that doctors would in future have to prescribe cheaper generic equivalents. In September 1983, health authorities were instructed to engage in competitive tendering for laundry, domestic, and catering services. Around the same time the deputizing service used by GPs also came under tighter control. Managerialism, having been placed firmly on the agenda, and preliminary skirmishes with the medical staff at operational levels having been begun on 3 February 1993, the Secretary of State announced that:

> Four leading businessmen are to conduct an independent management Inquiry into the effective use and management of manpower and related resources in the National Health Service . . . we are setting the Inquiry two main tasks: to examine the way in which resources are used and controlled inside the health service, so as to secure the best value for money and the best possible services for the patient [and] to identify what further management issues need pursuing for these important purposes . . .
>
> (DHSS 1983)

The original remit had extended well beyond the question of over-staffing. Expectations were high when the team reported only nine months later. The Griffiths Report, as it came to be known, contained a coherent critique of the weaknesses in current arrangements for managing the NHS. There were simple but telling points, such as the jibe that were Florence Nightingale walking through the wards she would certainly still be asking 'who is in charge?'. Griffiths noted change was difficult to achieve; the service was not geared up to implement new policies. Health output was not really considered, effectiveness in meeting needs was of secondary consideration to a seemingly steady stream of problems that drove a reactive style of management. Griffiths did not say so in so many words, but the disjuncture between levels of management, the implementors in the localities and the professionals at operational level was clearly in his mind when he recommended the appointment of a new class of general manager to take overall control of the service at regional, district/area and hospital levels.

As was apparent to contemporary commentators the changes proposed by Griffiths were radically different from the sort of political solutions that had been offered in the past. Symbolically, consensus management was abandoned and the new general managers encouraged to think of themselves as chief executives, there to take decisions in line with general policies set out by central government and adapted to local conditions by the lay boards that formally existed to provide health services for the communities they served. The Griffiths Report was also an opportunity to firm up the various managerialist devices and policies that had been devised over the past two years. Performance related pay and short-term contracts for senior managers was added to a list that included performance indicators and an annual review system for regions, districts and hospitals. For the first time in the history of the NHS a clear intention had been expressed to close the chain of command so as to link strategic management in Whitehall with the operational performance of the doctors on the wards. Clinical budgeting, re-named management budgeting, became identified as a central part of the process of change.

The impact of general management has been analysed extensively elsewhere by earlier researchers and attention is drawn to the perceived lack of behavioural change at operational level attributable to the 1984 reforms (Strong and Robinson 1990; Pettigrew *et al.* 1992). Harrison *et al.* concluded that, while local variations were considerable, the sum total of general management did not add up to a fundamental enough threat to demand a 'wholesale reassessment of the management-medicine interface'. The research team further concluded that locally successful general managers relied on softer interpersonal political skills rather than on techniques emphasized in management theory. This indicates the extent to which the initial impetus of the Griffiths Report failed to be carried on in the implementation stages where a feeling of 'business as usual' was allowed to prevail over the radical management agenda prescribed in 1983. In other words, Griffiths was implemented in an organization as yet uncured of the affliction of political accommodation (Harrison *et al.* 1992: 95–117).

The impact of individual components of the initiative such as performance indicators is difficult to judge. Suffice to say they failed to provide the ammunition needed by general managers to act as the change agents in the process of health care delivery in the UK. If general management did effect change then it did so in a self-limiting sort of way which did not close the managerial chain on operational levels of action driven by doctors in the hospitals. While the Griffiths Report had presented an insightful report, general management was really based on principles that had been hastily contrived from assumptions made about management practice in private industry. It was as if in 1984 the post-Griffiths leadership of the NHS refused to believe their eyes and assumed a management chain existed, where a strategy-forming elite could delegate implementation to managers in the localities who in turn would ensure operational conformance with central directives. Rather, the management task facing the NHS was required to begin with the creation of a working hierarchy for relaying instructions, since none existed below locality level management. By 1989 it was clear the general management reforms, while possibly robust enough in theoretical terms, were not enough to engineer together the profession-ally dominated operational level with the politically led management apparatus. Certainly the reforms had not been helped by a cool reaction from senior doctors in the hospitals. It became even clearer that the doctors did not work in a conventional organization with a chain of command – they could afford indifference. General management failed to gain suffi-cient momentum to cause change on its own.

3 Doctors and the market reforms

This chapter examines the impact of the internal market reforms initiated in 1989 on the roles played by doctors in the management process. The theory of the market is contrasted with its implementation. The chapter aims to provide a sense of the extent to which doctors have become *engaged* in the dynamics of the internal market in the mid-1990s, several years after the 1989 White Paper, Working for Patients.

Management by crisis in the 1990s

By 1989 it was clear that the general management reforms were not transforming the operational performance of the NHS. Politics had prevailed again. The vulnerability of the Conservatives to criticism over their stewardship of the NHS should not be underestimated. Yet the government may well have left the NHS alone but for the personal intervention of Margaret Thatcher. The issue of NHS funding had united the Labour opposition with the Royal Colleges and in 1987–9 a series of well co-ordinated attacks on ward closures, cancelled operations and rising waiting lists took place. The Prime Minister, whether by plan or in an act of spontaneity, announced a review of the NHS while being interviewed on the television programme *Panorama*. The review team, which was bolstered by the appointment of Kenneth Clarke as Health Secretary, reported directly to the Prime Minister. According to Timmins (1996: 472), the reform package that resulted was very nearly dropped by an anxious Prime Minister, influenced by her sceptical advisers and afraid of the consequences of failure in NHS reform.

While the internal market may not have been grounded in any experimentally based research, and as such was a doubtful means for addressing

the criticisms facing the NHS in the late 1980s, the market dynamic outlined in Working for Patients certainly equated well with the radical third-
term programme for privatization and de-regulation embarked on by the
Conservatives (Le Grand and Bartlett 1993: 1–12).

With quality and innovation as well as efficiency in focus the reforms
began to create separate organizations within the framework of a market,
in place of the 1948 vintage administrative apparatus (Department of
Health, Welsh Office and Scottish Home and Health Department 1989a).
From a strategic perspective the government was seemingly attempting to
effect behavioural change through promoting environmental change. If the
previous forty years had been dominated by administrative hierarchy and
medical profession-led operational practices, then exposing the activity of
managers in the localities and doctors in hospitals and medical centres to
an environment conditioned by market forces should, so the theory went,
in turn cause fundamental behavioural change of a type previously
unachievable at operational levels. On the face of it, the government had
given up the idea of managing a chain of command. In the previous
chapter the lack of inclination to close the chain on medical activity was
discussed at length. Working for Patients seemed to be saying that rather
than use managerialist devices to control doctors' activities, market forces
would provide the mixture of discipline and incentive the NHS needed to
control its core professional employees. The key was in establishing a
market environment and a price-quality sensitivity at every level (Hunter
1993: 38–40).

Achieving consistency of strategic direction at every level in the NHS
involves massive cultural change. Managers and doctors had to be made
to believe that their environment had changed – almost an act of faith. On
an institutional level there is indeed a good deal of obvious change. It is
immediately apparent that in contrast with previous reforms, Working for
Patients included the medical profession in its design to a far greater
extent. Attention can be drawn to the changing roles of health authorities,
the establishment of self-governing hospital trusts and the growing prominence of General Practice Fundholding. The precise implications for
medical management and the way doctors carry out their work are less
apparent.

Principles of the internal market

The key concept of the internal market was the separation of the functions
of purchasing and service delivery. Prior to the reforms, the health authorities (or boards in Scotland) had been responsible for the overall provision
of secondary and some primary health care to populations within their
area. Family practitioner committees and health boards in Scotland existed
to channel the resources needed to fund the primary services provided by
GPs, dentists, pharmacists and opticians. A hierarchy existed whereby the
health authorities devolved responsibilities for the day-to-day management

of hospitals to unit managers. The primary health care sector related to the secondary sector through the actions on the part of GPs in referring patients to consultants in the hospital units. This was essentially a professional interaction which was not subject to managerial control in any direct sense. Usage made by GPs of referrals to the secondary care sector was of course limited by the funds made available by health authorities to pay for hospital services. The environment they operated in may be said to have been conditioned by rationing. This is management of resources through forming queues and is a means of controlling access to health services and therefore costs, consistent with the 'hands-off' type of management adopted in the NHS for the first thirty or so years of its existence.

The environment post-Working for Patients is, by contrast, theoretically market choice driven. Consequent implications for the medical profession are immense. Underpinning the introduction of the internal market was the belief that choice, efficiency and quality within the health service would be encouraged by competition between provider units for contracts from purchasers. Trusts are not supposed to ration access to health care. Rather they must strive to meet a profitability target (currently 6 per cent on turnover) which means securing the business in the form of contracts from purchasers – both Health Authorities and GP fundholders. Given certain limitations on the structure of the market they operate in, they are theoretically in more or less direct competition with other rival trusts. For instance, Raigmore NHS Trust in Inverness has limited realistic competition given its remote location whereas an NHS trust in Manchester has over twenty competitors offering broadly equivalent ranges of services within the Greater Manchester conurbation.

Hospital-based doctors are the professionals ultimately responsible for service delivery in secondary care. Their actions largely determine the costs and quality of services provided. As such the successful management of their performance ought to be the central factor determining a provider unit's position in the marketplace. However, Working for Patients was an exercise in redefining the environment which doctors and other health professionals work in and should not in itself be considered as a programme in management reform. Consequently, only a few paragraphs of the White Paper are devoted to the managerial role of doctors in the new NHS. The market merely implies a role for doctors as key players in a competitive process. In any market the central dynamic is provided by competition, when markets work smoothly it will be impossible for a seller of goods or services to charge more than the 'market price' for any length of time. To do so will invite competitors, either existing or prospective, to enter the market and swallow up the expensive sellers' share. This simple mechanism based on a constant threat from the purchaser to buy someone else's product, provides a strong lever against costly inefficient behaviour on the part of producers.

Two central management roles are thus demanded. One is concerned with curbing clinical behaviour that could lead to the producer charging too much for the service provided. The second is a purchasing management function. In this latter case, purchasers must seek the cheapest price for the product they want or they fail to attain maximum welfare gains from the transaction they are entering into. Therefore the post-Working for Patients NHS ought to, as a first priority, have developed a management structure that ensured these fundamental tasks were accomplished. Policy makers ought to retain responsibility for making sure the market signals are strong enough for managers to respond to, either as producers or purchasers. Success or failure ought to be judged on the extent to which managers of provider units succeed in either driving down the costs of 'products' or building enhanced quality into the product at no price increase, or marketing new products. The signals that purchasers are making about their perceptions of price and quality on offer have to be communicated successfully in order that providers may react appropriately (Maynard 1993a: 58–68).

The idea of an internal market was triply attractive to the Conservative government. Politically markets and competition appealed to the right of the party and Working for Patients fitted comfortably with the grand plan for de-regulating and rolling back the state. Secondly, the market mechanisms promised greater efficiency and innovation. Thirdly, the market was internal, the state was not actually giving up its ability to place limits on the global expenditure on health care. (The absence of global controls being the major weakness in the US health care system (Spurgeon 1993: 46–8).)

In this scheme doctors would be exposed to the rigours and incentives of the marketplace as purchasers and providers, while operating under the umbrella of the public sector. Doctors would deal with the micromanagement task of curbing expensive behaviour and responding to incentives to improve clinical quality and act innovatively.

Doctors as purchasers and managers of resources

Central to the implementation of the NHS reforms has been the concept of general practice fundholding. While beginning slowly, with reservations among doctors clearly evident, fundholding has gradually become the dominant status in general practice (Glennerster *et al.* 1994: 54–73). Fundholding involves allocating an annual budget to General Practices that meet certain core organizational criteria, specifically relating to size and management capability. The budget provides a resource pool from which fundholders have to purchase certain types of care from providers in both the public or private sectors. Budgets initially covered elective surgical treatment, out-patient services and diagnostic investigations, together with prescribed drugs and certain practice costs (Department of Health, Welsh Office and Scottish Home and Health Department 1989b). However, since April 1993, the budget has also included a community element, from which GPs must purchase a range of community health services. Health Boards or District Health Authorities continue to purchase these services on behalf of those practices which are not fundholders.

The rationale behind giving General Practices control of their own budgets was that such a scheme would:

> ... offer GPs an opportunity to improve the quality of services on offer to patients, stimulate hospitals to be more responsive to the needs of GPs and their patients and to develop their own practices for the benefit of their patients.
>
> (Social Services Committee 1989: 19)

By 1994 it was effectively possible for any practice to take the fundholding route. Restrictions which had prohibited fundholding where a practice's list was less than 11,000 were changed to allow practices with 7000 patients to apply, and for smaller practices or single practitioners to group together to make an application. The experimental nature of fundholding has also allowed practices to enter into consortia with other practices for the purposes of striking better deals with provider units. In addition, there is also the experiment with 'total fundholding' where a small number of practices have taken on the entire health care budget for their list including elective work, accident and emergency services and health promotion.

Nevertheless, given the necessary qualification that has to be made for the restricted market opportunities in certain localities, fundholding does hold out the possibility of GP managed gains in several different aspects of primary care. In summing up the potential impact of fundholding Glennerster (1994: 45–9) suggests the following criteria should be used.

Hospital efficiency and responsiveness

Glennerster believes experience is showing that GPs have greater motivation than health authorities when it comes to seeking better contracts. The GPs have better information about the service quality on offer and it is the fundholders rather than district-based purchasers who have been prepared to diversify their choice of providers and threaten to shift contracts to competitors.

Allocative efficiency between sectors

GP fundholders are said to have the incentive to work on optimizing the allocative balance between resources used to treat patients in the primary, secondary and community care sectors. As has already been argued, the barriers between the health care sectors were constructed for political convenience rather than for reasons of medical effectiveness or administrative efficiency. Glennerster sees fundholding as the catalyst for GPs to find innovative ways of treating patients which may in certain cases dismiss with the standard process of referring patients on to the secondary sector. It is not hard to find excellent examples of innovative patient care among fundholding GPs. For example, one practice the author has worked with became aware of an orthopaedics service being offered by a GP in a nearby practice. The service was based on therapeutic principles and provided a direct alternative to surgery for some patients. On the basis that less than half the patients referred to orthopaedic surgeons were actually deemed suitable for operations the therapeutic service was an attractive alternative course of action. Many fundholders now carry out minor operations and arrange for specialist clinics to be held in their surgeries, once again breaking with the traditional referral pattern altogether. Evidence regarding the health economic impact of such changes is not yet generally available.

Practice efficiency

Glennester believes 'better practice management' has resulted as a by-product of fundholding. Fundholding does imply a need for stricter administrative discipline.

Economy on drugs

Fundholders were given a particular incentive to find ways of reducing prescribing costs. Savings made under this budget heading may be ploughed back into other areas of expenditure.

Administrative costs

There is a basic principle in all economic analysis that 'transaction' costs, that is those resources that must be devoted to making a trade, must not outweigh benefits of the exchange between buyer and seller. In fundholding terms this means that the efforts of GPs devoted to locating the best providers must not cost more than the net gain to the patient and the NHS as a whole. Glennerster acknowledges that practice-based contracting is going to cost more in administrative terms than will the same process carried out by district-based organizations. His team concluded, however, that the better individualized patient information available to GPs outweighed administrative costs.

The scale of referrals

It has long been acknowledged that unjustifiable variations exist in the number of referrals made by GPs. Theoretically, fundholding ought to provide an incentive for GPs to scrutinize referrals and think twice about sending patients to see a specialist as a matter of routine. In practice, this is not an immediately obvious outcome. Glennerster identifies the 'historic'-based budget setting system as being at fault. Practices have their budgets set on the basis of existing referral patterns, which is said to undermine their enthusiasm for change. Glennerster advocates a capitation system of budget setting. This would involve using a formula for allocating budgets to practices on the basis of the patient list characteristics in terms of age, deprivation and so on.

Comprehensive planning

Glennerster sees fundholding as providing a modern basis for replacing an out-dated planning system which has traditionally been based on epidemiological calculations of district population health needs. The business of 'scientific' planning had little time for consumer preferences and patient demand. He argues that retailers such as Sainsburys are not tempted to impose consumption patterns on their customers, so why should the NHS? Glennerster sees fundholding GPs as the agents for channelling consumer preference into the planning process where a balance can be struck between 'medical need' and 'patient demand'.

Health of the Nation

The most recent statement of health priorities identified key areas: for targeting coronary heart disease, strokes, cancer, mental illness, HIV/AIDS, accidents and special health needs of elderly, poor and ethnic members of society. One argument sees district led coordination as the only means of making ground towards specific health targets and fundholding as fragmentary and divisive. Glennerster however, points out that since 1993 'Health of the Nation' targets have been part of the instructions on performance given to fundholders.

Accountability

Fundholders are allowed to use savings made on their fund to invest in any aspect of the practice. As practice premises and the bulk of practice equipment are owned by the GPs there is clear scope for fundholders to make personal financial gains when selling on a share in a partnership. Accountability questions are therefore raised by the fundholding arrangement.

Budget volatility

It is quite legitimate to ask who steps in when fundholders go over budget. Safeguards of sorts are in place but inevitably financial mis-management will occur, particularly when fundholding is extended to cover emergency cases.

Fundholding and the development of the management role in General Practice

Few GPs have had their working patterns and clinical practices transformed by fundholding. Of more importance for many fundholding and non-fundholding GPs has been the imposition of new contractual relations with the NHS. Ahead of the implementation of fundholding, a new contract for GPs came into operation on 1 April 1990. Establishing a clearer definition of the responsibilities and services to be provided by general practices, the contract also introduced financial incentives for doctors to meet preventative medicine targets in areas such as vaccinations and cervical smears. While implemented without a great deal of consultation the new contract has been seen to meet some long-standing flaws in the system of primary health care management.

The General Practice is typically a small- to medium-sized business, with anything up to twenty partners. All practices now employ a practice manager. The new contract helped establish some basic management principles, particularly in the areas of record keeping and finance. Practice lists and numbers of partners have grown since 1948, practices now have nurses, health visitors and mid-wives attached to them. In the contract were contained incentives for practices to provide special clinics for minor surgery and encouragement to pay greater attention to effective management of patients with chronic diseases such as asthma. The introduction of indicative prescribing budgets also encouraged GPs to adopt a more proactive approach to their use of resources.

Finally, the medical audit was established as a basic principle in the management of general practice. Medical audit in primary care dates back to the 1970s but has been given a renewed impetus in the context of the internal market. The 1989 White Paper, Working for Patients required each Family Health Service Authority (FHSA) to set up a Medical Audit Advisory Group (MAAG) to direct and coordinate clinical audit activity in primary care (Department of Health, Welsh Office and Scottish Home and Health Department 1989c).

Initially, it appeared that the government was prepared to go down the path of regulating GP performance by using audit as a device for identifying outlier behaviour. For instance, the propensity of some GPs to refer more frequently than their practice colleagues would in performance indicator terms place them in the position of statistical outliers from the mean referral rate. Working Paper 6 of Working for Patients, dealt with audit, defining it thus: 'the systematic, critical analysis of medical care, including the procedures used for diagnosis and treatment, and the resulting outcome and quality of life for the patient'. The link between management and audit was hinted at but not developed, the stress in the document being on the need for the task to be led by physicians – 'external audit by peers in general practice'. The task of audit was therefore to be undertaken by clinicians, the government having retreated from the potentially confrontational position of establishing FHSAs as the auditing body. Instead a new organization was created in the form of the District Medical Audit Advisory Group to oversee audit (Department of Health 1990). Unlike in secondary care, where audit became a contractual requirement for consultants, GPs have participated on a voluntary basis. With little in the way of central guidelines or precedent to follow, each MAAG has developed its own approach (Lawrence 1993; Spencer 1993).

Primary care: GPs as innovators

If the first wave of successful applications for fundholding included a high number of pro-market GPs, successive cohorts may be more influenced by the freedoms to develop a new primary health care agenda which can be summarized as follows:

- provision of new clinical services
- consumerism and professional standards
- health promotion and health targets
- improving and assuring quality
- teamworking with other health professionals
- service delivery opportunities arising from fundholding
- developments in partnership arrangements and GP contracts. (Williamson 1992; Irvine 1993; Munro 1993; Willis 1993; Bowie and Harris 1994)

This is an agenda which is at least partly shared by non-fundholding GPs. The extent to which the fundholding experience has quickened change in primary care is unproven. Fundholding, on the other hand, has undoubtedly caused many practices to examine their own management systems and also sharpened up partners' sense of their resource use responsibilities.

The success of fundholding depends on the abilities of GPs to use resources more effectively. Attention to prescribing, for example, may produce savings. Nevertheless, the efforts of GPs acting as individuals are likely to be of limited impact. To achieve gains requires GPs to perform as part of a team. Within the practice this means working with medical colleagues as well as nurses, midwives, health visitors and administrative staff. Progress has been made in many practices under a range of initiatives often involving the Royal College of General Practitioners, which have focused attention on the performance of the primary health care team. The clearer responsibility for resource use associated with fundholding appears to encourage partners to examine their managerial practices within their systems.

However, fundholding has also been particularly significant in exposing holes in the overall management system that links the primary care sector to the secondary care sector. Plamping and Fischer (1994: 22–3) argue that before fundholding, the General Practice did not have to relate to the rest of the health care system as an organization. Certainly relations with hospital doctors were traditionally conducted on an individual basis, mainly through the referral letter system where notes are exchanged between GP and consultant. This has changed with the fundholding practice as an entity now contracting with provider units, although it has not necessarily produced significant changes in the way the two sectors combine. For example, the gains to be made through setting up new 'outreach' clinics where specialists will work in the health centres may be of great significance. The incentives are apparent, but perhaps as Plamping and Fischer claim, are outweighed by the inhibiting factors still left in the system post-Working for Patients. GPs remain self-employed and the General Medical Service contract is still practitioner based not practice based. General Medical Service money (the budget allocated by the health authority to the practice) is seen by GPs as their money as of rights, instead of a pool of resources they are managing on behalf of a population. This in turn is said to inhibit co-operation with provider units, in the sense that practices cannot see an immediate reason to allow trusts to use their General Medical Service money as part of a service package. It might be advantageous, for example, to use practice-based resources in post-operative care in place of trust resources in the form of out-patient care, as long as they remain self-employed practitioners with a personal financial investment in a practice. The implication is that behavioural change on the part of GPs leading to innovative networks would be more likely to occur if GPs were paid on a different basis, one which reduced their personal financial risk.

The re-designation of GPs as purchasers also provided an opportunity to adjust the balance of power between them and hospital-based consultants. On accepting their role within the NHS in 1948, GPs had lost a considerable degree of professional status and power to hospital-based consultants (Honigsbaum 1979: 301–14). The hospital specialists no longer had to court GPs for private patients. Consultants, now freed of the need to attract private patients for their income, could afford to pay less attention to relationships with their professional colleagues in primary care. Relations could and did in many cases become fairly slight with little communication taking place beyond that formally required in the sending of letters through the referral process. Referral letters vary greatly in quality of content. Roland (1992: 108–9) suggests that the hospital consultants, in short, had little compulsion pre-Working for Patients to treat GPs as 'customers'. Post-1990 the fundholding GP should in theory have the financial leverage to demand fuller attention from the consultant when making a referral. Glennerster *et al.* (1994: 91–5) claimed that purchasers, especially GP fundholders, have already demonstrated an ability to exert an influence over providers in relation to service delivery. Cost, quality and innovation are the three areas which the new market-invigorated relationship between purchasers and providers is expected to realize gains.

NHS trusts and managing hospital doctors

The White Paper, Working for Patients, committed the government to 'devolving decision-making in the NHS to local operational level'. One fundamental development was the opportunity given to the staff of hospitals and other units to apply for self-governing status, which would give them operational independence from health authorities. Self-governing units would take on the separate legal identity of an NHS trust. The medical profession were scripted into the corporate hierarchy of these new organizations. Trusts are required to appoint a board of directors consisting of a chief executive, director of finance, medical representative and nursing representative as executive members and an equal number of non-executive directors, with a further non-executive appointee chairing the board. (It is common for a further executive, often in charge of human resources, to sit on the board. This addition must be balanced by a further non-executive appointment.) Trust boards typically comprise eleven members. This makes them considerably smaller than the old-style health authorities. The formal political position is that non-executive members, including the chairman, are appointed by the Secretary of State solely on the basis of the contribution they can make to the management of the provider unit. The NHS Management Executive (NHSME) encouraged individuals to put their names forward for appointment to trust boards through the medium of advertising. It is thought that many of the directors come from business backgrounds (Bartlett and Le Grand 1994).

The size and composition of trust boards were in keeping with the principle of running provider units on business lines. The non-executive directors, two of which were to be drawn from the local community, had to be able to demonstrate an orientation towards the management task. Trusts receive no direct funding from the Management Executive and must theoretically earn all their income through competitive processes. Trusts are expected to contract for the provision of health care services with health boards, GP fundholders and private patients or their insurers on the basis of price and quality. To allow them to compete for patients, the board of directors were vested with a 'range of powers and freedoms' not available to existing NHS health authorities and hospitals:

- the power to acquire, own and dispose of assets to ensure the most effective use of them;
- the ability to make a case for capital development;
- the power to borrow, primarily for new building and equipment, subject to an annual financing limit;
- freedom to retain operating surpluses and build up reserves;
- freedom to set their own management structures without control from areas or the Management Executive;
- freedom to employ a mix of staff on terms they consider appropriate;
- freedom to determine pay and conditions of services for staff, and to conduct their own industrial relations;
- freedom to employ and direct their own medical and nursing staff;
- freedom to advertise their services. (Department of Health, Welsh Office and Scottish Home and Health Department 1989c) (NHS Management Executive – Scottish Home and Health Department 1991)

These specific new freedoms were to be granted in an environment that was promised to be considerably less conditioned by instructions and guidance issued by central government. In terms of financial duties the board of directors were compelled to achieve a 6 per cent return on assets in use, break even annually on their income and expenditure account and stay within an external financing limit. The Scottish Management Executive's guide for Scottish trusts states that accounts should be 'commercial in style' (NHS in Scotland Management Executive 1991).

The inter-linked management challenges of developing adequate operational cost information systems and exerting control over the medical profession became immediate problems for the boards of the new trusts. The implications for the doctors employed in trusts as the professionals responsible for delivering services in this new commercial environment were considerable, yet unspecified. With contractual changes implemented in 1993 consultants may now have their contracts held with the trust instead of being employed by regional health authorities in England or health boards in Scotland. These new contractual arrangements may yet prove significant. However, chief executives had little of immediate substance to draw on in their task of controlling doctors' performance. General management had been launched as a system for closing the management chain. It implied, but never realized, closer control of clinicians and their use of resources in patient care. The 'general management' system that was implemented was actually still respectful of the traditional administrative-medical boundaries of control and influence. As commentators have remarked, sailing without compass and rudder is a dangerous if not hopeless business. The internal market, with the threat of lost business due to a lack of control over clinical behaviour, placed resource use and quality/cost control much further up the 'real agenda'.

Managing doctors in the trusts

According to King *et al.*, the 1989 White Paper presented new pressures on providers of health care to:

- generate the costs of specific services offered for the marketplace,
- challenge existing assumptions about the efficiency of services offered, to maintain competitive standards, and
- assist in the construction of budgets which are sensitive to changes in the mix of services offered to the market. (King *et al.* 1994)

The two key instruments of control set out in the White Paper were a re-launched resource management initiative and medical audit. The resource management initiative or 'management budgeting mark III', seemed to be a critical piece in the internal market jigsaw. As Spurgeon (1993: 87) has written, it seemed that finally the clinicians and managers would be brought together by a system for monitoring and controlling service outputs and costed inputs. The resource management initiative was to provide the NHS with a system for managing the set of resource consuming processes involved in treating patients. Drawing on the work undertaken in the six pilot sites set up in the 1980s the 'roll-out' would, according to the Department, emphasize clinician involvement in the generation and use of data, the quality dimension as opposed to cost reduction, the opportunity to develop realistic and accurate case-mix and costing systems from which robust comparisons of resource utilization could be made.

The resource management initiative represented an attempt to extend budgeting responsibility down to the level of the individual hospital consultant. Packwood and colleagues identified four key elements in the resource management initiative (Packwood *et al.* 1991: 13). First, the doctors, nurses and paramedics who directly treat and care for patients should become attuned to information describing the effectiveness of different patterns of treatment; secondly, consultants whose decisions commit resources should be involved in planning resource use; thirdly, there should be a focus on identifying the effects of existing resource use and alternatives; and fourthly, stronger control of resources should result from rational and responsible management and use of information. The resource management initiative fully implemented therefore constitutes a powerful proactive tool for the leaders of the NHS trusts.

Audit and hospital doctors

The 1989 White Paper also firmly established audit of patient care as a responsibility for hospital doctors (Department of Health 1989d). The logic of carrying out audits whereby patient care processes are benchmarked according to performance criteria and subjected to a regular review is fairly clear, given the importance that quality and costs should play in a competitive internal market. Ring-fenced funds were provided to support the development of audit in hospitals in recognition of the importance being attached to the process in the broader context of organizational reform. Audit is a process with a lengthy history in certain specialities such as obstetrics. In other specialties the requirements of the NHS Act 1990 have demanded that processes be started more or less from scratch. As in the primary care sector the Department did not stipulate either the form that audit should take or define the terms through which audit was to be integrated with the management process. As a consequence, the impact of medical audit has been very varied. Kerrison *et al.* reported on the experience of four hospitals with audit to 1993. Their conclusions are not encouraging from a management perspective. While audit does seem to produce changes in medical practice, encourage the production of local standards and provide a good educational tool within specialty training programmes, there is little direct linkage with the broader management processes in the hospitals. Audit has been allowed to remain a medical dominated business, often being dependent and therefore influenced by particular consultants. While audit committees were established in the hospitals, no sense of a chain of command existed. Doctors participated in audit on a fairly casual basis picking the subjects they wanted to examine rather than being directed by either colleagues or the hospital managers. Concern with technical aspects of medical care have dominated the audit process with relatively little interest shown in resource use as a problem to be examined.

The idea that the post-White Paper implementation of audit was compromised by 'politics', and has failed to develop in any significant way as a management tool, is reflected in the more recent attempt by the NHS Executive (1994) to change the sense of purpose underlying audit. In consequence, the term clinical audit is now preferred to medical audit, signifying that audit is not an exercise that can be confined exclusively to the direct work of doctors but must instead be focused on the process of patient care in which the medical profession is central, but highly dependent on an often lengthy list of team players drawn from many professional backgrounds. In addition, the views of purchasers have been emphasized in the Executive demand for more effort to go into 'interface audit'. The prospects for integrating the work carried out under the label of audit within general management of trusts is examined in Chapter 5.

Improvization

The reality of the resource management initiative is far from impressive. Spurgeon has concluded that even the beginnings of the information revolution is some way off. Where systems have been set up they are still not used properly. Managers do not seem to trust quantitative information when it concerns clinical care, while the doctors find it hard to incorporate resource management data into clinical decisions. Too often technological aspects dominate systems to the exclusion of actual usage of information management capabilities. Data is plentiful but analysis and responses are scarce in the new NHS.

Significantly, the resource management initiative has rarely provoked much conflict between management and doctors in hospitals. This may serve to indicate the lack of status accorded to this potentially important tool by both managers and doctors alike. It is questionable whether the management of the NHS and particularly the management of doctors can undergo real change in the sense of making directed efforts towards strategic goals through the influencing of clinical practice. Medical audit has tended to be thought of by doctors as a worthy exercise on grounds of the opportunities afforded to carry out research on interesting aspects of practice and for the contribution it may make to the education of colleagues. The optimism of the 1989 working paper on medical audit regarding the integration of audit with management was misplaced. Consultants have not 'naturally' come round to see audit as a management tool. In spite of the prominence and financial support accorded to audit in the 1989 White

Paper, little progress is being made towards using this system for corporate purposes of adding value to the effectiveness of clinical practice.

Market signals: the limitations of GPs as purchasers

The Glennerster vision is of a health service driven by the primary care providers – not a closing of the chain between policy and operations, but an abandonment of the whole notion of hierarchy. This involves a considerable faith in the market mechanism and in particular the adoption of a proactive management role to be taken up by GPs and purchasing bodies in their capacity as the patient's agent in the choice of provider. The extent of market-led adjustment in GP's patterns of referral to competing provider units is debatable, Glennerster and his colleagues expressed considerable optimism about the impact of fundholding on choice on the basis of a study of GPs in London. The purchaser-provider market in London is, however, very much a 'best case'. GPs have more hospitals to choose from within easy travelling distance than in any other part of the country. Perhaps of even more significance is the extent to which London practice lists are composed of people with relatively little ties with particular neighbourhoods and local hospitals, making it easier for GPs to send them to a hospital out of the area. This can be contrasted with other parts of the country where loyalty to particular hospitals is often very strong and a sense of reluctance to send patients to competitor units high among GPs. In certain areas competition is impractical because of distances from 'alternative' providers.

In the mid-1990s, the cost of individual treatments was not seemingly an important factor in fundholders' referral judgements. The structure of budgets based as they were on the practice's historical resource use and referral patterns was not forcing GPs to shop around. Simple monetary comparisons could be dismissed as a basis for making referrals to alternative providers. The impact of GPs acting as health care 'agents' on behalf of their patients is instead dependent on the professional decision-making processes used (Marnoch *et al.* 1996). GPs will tend to rank the consultant as the most important factor in making a referral decision. Small numbers of GPs may have a formal system for choosing a consultant – for example, they keep a database on the individual consultants they have used in the past, recording their perceptions of strengths and weaknesses. However, this degree of formality in the collection of information is unusual. Most GPs keep information 'in their heads'. The quality of knowledge of the existence and attractiveness of alternative providers is variable. Information tends to be gathered in a fairly haphazard fashion. Medical 'grapevines' are a common source of informally conveying information. More formally, hospital departments have open days, where GPs are invited to visit departments and meet the staff. When a new consultant is appointed there is frequently an effort made on the part of the new person to let GPs hear about their interests and particular skills. GPs will also frequently know a group of consultants from their training period in a local hospital. Patients are another source of information on consultant's performance, and their views are sometimes actively sought by GPs as part of a decision-making process on where to refer future patients. Many GPs expect an informative post-consultation letter from specialists and will take note of those individuals who are poor correspondants.

While GPs may not retain a very detailed knowledge of consultants they can readily identify individuals who they see to be underperforming, and who have failed to meet their standards in the past. 'Experience' is based on 'professional judgement' and is not dependent on a precise quantified calculation. GPs tend to have an 'acceptable range' into which a consultant's work must fall or else they shift referrals elsewhere. GPs will break a referral relationship when quality, for whatever reason, falls outside the acceptable range. This acceptable range is not readily articulated and is very probably defined according to different criteria on a more or less individual basis. The relationship between consultant and GP is mostly stable but subject to abrupt termination when an invisible line is breached. The performance of the hospital in terms of its organizational capacity to provide follow-up treatment and quality in-patient care is seemingly subject to the same type of judgement.

In spite of high political significance and media attention, comparison of waiting times is of less significance to those GPs with a real choice of where to refer a patient to than might have been expected. For many, it is difficult to argue that waiting time comparison is routinely part of their referral process. Part of the reason may be the relative inaccuracy of waiting times bulletins and the poor presentation of information by provider units.

GPs are similar to purchasers in many other service areas in that they appreciate the personal costs of time and effort involved in identifying alternative suppliers. The flow of information in the NHS is still based to a large extent on informal channels. As decision makers GPs, like other professionals, routinely rely on heuristics or 'rules of thumb' in arriving at decisions. GPs are typically 'risk averse', they understand the nature of risk in sending patients to new untried provider units. Consequently, there has to be a clear advantage to be gained in terms of quality of service or speed of treatment before they will enter into full analysis of the relative claims made by alternative providers. Adopting more complex choice processes is not obviously worthwhile in the NHS at present (Laing and Cotton 1995: 583–600). Health gains are not immediately realizable by the process of shifting providers.

Financial management

The link between financial control systems and management behaviour in the NHS has been explored by MacKerrell (1993: 146–59). The centre has been seen to be less enthusiastic about devolving financial control than might have been anticipated in 1989. Progress with the resource management initiative was stalled by the conflict that had arisen between the medical profession and the government over Working for Patients. These are factors that may have influenced the initial construction of financial information systems by NHS general managers and directors of finance. The accounting regime established by the NHSME was devised in a climate where the desire to experiment with trading relationships was waning, hence a consequent lack of focus on developing appropriate financial systems.

The NHS financial control system is based on the following standard principles:

• prices should be based on costs
• costs should be arrived at on a full cost basis
• there should be no planned cross-subsidization between contracts.

The implications of the current financial control regime are there to see. NHS provider units are expected to attribute fixed and variable costs to individual specialties and then divide by the number of episodes undertaken to come up with 'average specialty costs' or cost per episode. (A finished consultant episode is a medical profession conceived unit.) MacKerrell describes this as a version of industries' concept of 'prime costs'. He also points out that industry does not generally use full cost pricing. Pricing is market led to a greater or lesser extent.

MacKerrell contends that financial control systems can influence:

• the enthusiasm of customers, by the level of prices set;
• the behaviour of colleagues, by the method of apportioning indirect costs for pricing purposes;
• the structure of the organization, by the design of the internal-control systems.

The type of financial control system adopted by an organization ought to be contingent on the circumstances facing it. The internal market invited radical developments in financial control.

Unfortunately, the NHSME, whether by accident or by design, have created a system of financial control that is not suitable as a management technology for a competitive business environment. For example, full cost pricing was used in the defence sector where in the 'golden days' of cold war budgets, manufacturers tallied up all the research and development, design and production costs and passed them on to the government procurers in defence departments as cost plus a profit margin. The accounting regime was not expected to be a tool for management to use in its scrutiny and control over its designers' and engineers' behaviour, nor was it much connected with organizational structure in any direct sense. Defence contractors knew they were not in a competitive market where price levels had to be 'right' or else it would not be possible to sell the missile system, and they reacted accordingly in their choice of financial control system. The purchasers for their part had no need to disagree with this response.

The UK's Ministry of Defence, for example, was budget limited like other spending departments in Whitehall and its primary aim was to meet procurement targets within a politically determined spending cycle. Political requirements to keep a large domestic defence manufacturing capacity ruled out the Ministry of Defence's entering the international defence procurement market as a cost-sensitive consumer. The organizational analogy with the politically sensitive health care sector will be apparent. The NHS is operating under a similar regime where the twin goals of global cost control and political stability (not allowing hospitals to be too successful or too unsuccessful in winning contracts) are more important than using the financial control system to stimulate market-orientated behaviour. This includes setting the right price to allow for a strategy of growth in a particular specialty, or helping management identify expensive behaviour on the part of consultants.

Seen in this light it is easier to explain why the high profile creation of the clinical directorates system and all the contracting activity and mergers that have gone on over the last five years has not been accompanied by major changes in the way clinicians behave in resource management terms. That the full-cost pricing system does not provide a tool for managers in a market trading relationship is becoming apparent. MacKerrell notes that although 40 per cent of the average NHS unit's expenditures fall into the category of 'overheads' no standard procedure has been stipulated for apportioning these costs between procedures performed by specialties. Not unexpectedly in a huge organization like the NHS, local priorities have resulted in widely varying calculations for apportioning costs. MacKerrell refers to a damning report by Elwood for the Chartered Institute of Management Accountants which reported that a consultant episode in obstetrics can vary in cost from £350 to £1353 between provider units. Approximately 40 per cent of costs cannot be attributed directly to a consultant episode, so to put a price on a particular course of clinical intervention requires a judgement to be made on how indirect costs are to be shared out between specialties. Because no standard rule exists, when calculations are made for costing a clinical procedure there is a considerable variation in the system used by trusts for apportioning indirect costs. The production of a protocol for identifying direct costs associated with clinical procedures and an appropriate share of indirect costs would be expensive and organizationally challenging. It would, however, form a more robust financial base for the internal market. The resource management initiative was to be rolled-out in the Working for Patients reform process. Not much progress has been made here, however, signifying the low priority of making market signals accurately reflect clinical efficiency and economy in political terms. Total expenditure is of prime importance and this continues to dominate financial control at every level of the NHS. In such a context it is of far less importance than might have been thought in 1990, for managers to use accounting devices to focus attention on the resource consuming behaviour of clinicians, and to design organizational control systems to meet the pricing sensitivities of the internal market.

Political fright

District health authorities (DHAs) were theoretically allowed to choose between competing provider units. In reality they virtually always chose their former district units. The element of choice was more formal than real. In placing a contract it is unlikely that a DHA would discover one hospital was better than its competitors across the range of clinical specialties. It would therefore pay to spread contracts across a number of provider units locating the best services in terms of price and quality. This in turn would inevitably mean that bare patches would occur in the provider units' range of provision in circumstances where they found themselves no longer able to maintain a service in particular specialties when the contract had been lost. Here we could anticipate that political constraints would start to be applied. Could government really allow a situation to arise where, for example, in a large city no neurosurgery could be offered by the local hospital? Patients would in effect be sent to another locality for this work. Even more alarmingly some units might find they lose out on a number of contracts to competitors threatening the viability of the unit as a whole. Would government be prepared to allow geographical gaps to appear in hospital coverage? As it happened neither of these scenarios became reality. Was this because managers of provider units put pressure on their physicians to react to the trading relationship and modify their behaviour to compete on price and quality? Or was it because a 'steady state' approach was demanded by government which denied the electorally damaging possibility of services disappearing and hospitals closing? The answer is obvious to anyone connected with the management of the NHS. Those managers responsible for DHA purchasing knew they were not just expected to go out and get the best possible deal for their populations. There were political criteria to be considered as well. In the first four years of the internal market little pressure was brought to bear on the physicians as a consequence of the need for the managers of their units to get competitive services operating in their departments.

As of 1 April 1994, however, the context of the trading relationship began to change significantly with DHA purchasing beginning to be matched more closely by purchasing done by GP fundholders in some localities. It would seem that GPs are more promising purchasers. First, they are taking resource utilization decisions on behalf of a list of patients amounting to perhaps around 600 referrals a year as opposed to an entire population of a district. As a result the dangerous consequences of monopoly purchaser decisions are removed at a stroke. The viability of provider units is not under threat in the same way as before where a single decision by a DHA could theoretically have closed down a hospital. Management of the purchasing side of the trading relationship becomes politically acceptable.

As Saltmann and Otter (1992: 22) recognized, the initial emphasis of 'multiple market style mechanisms' had been toned down and the centre quickly reasserted its prerogatives of financial control. 'Entrepreneurial behaviour' on the part of NHS managers had to be conducted within a familiarly strict regime. It is fair to conclude that much of the glisten of market relationships had been tarnished by the BMAs campaign against the internal market on a national level and the expressions of alarm communicated by doctors up and down the country. Whether they act accordingly or not, it has become an act of worship for managers in some large private sector corporations to repeat the catechism about 'people being our greatest resource'. The implementation of the NHS reforms verified their faith in a negative sort of way. The internal market core of the reforms needed to be quickly translated into actual behavioural change on the part of doctors, conditioned by the need to respond to trading relationships. That this has as yet failed to happen probably signifies the failure of the initial Working for Patients reform package. Policies either tend to be implemented in the first three to four years of their lives or be supplanted by a new set of ideas. The internal market as a live concept whose impact could not be predicted was killed off at the first opportunity by the Department of Health/Management Executive. The presence of an arch-pragmatist in the figure of the Secretary of State Kenneth Clarke probably accelerated the demise of the internal market dynamic as a focus for change. To invite or even demand entrepreneurial actions on the part of professionals at the front line of the NHS is dangerous. They could make mistakes or be demonstrably successful, both of which are outcomes that impart an element of disorder into the system. If 'entrepreneurial activity' could be limited to the domain of the general managers then it could still be controlled by the centre. Perhaps this was the calculation made in 1990–91.

Future of the market

Management by crisis could not be sustained in a politically constituted health care system. In this chapter it has been argued that the initial shock of the market was quickly absorbed by the health service culture such that a seemingly radical organizational restructuring of the management-medical interface based on the clinical directorates model could actually be used to support a preservation of traditional boundaries of decision making and control. Yet the forces for change have not gone away. Even in an NHS tired of organizational upheaval there remains the need to enact organizational change to exploit developments in clinical practice and respond to demands for choice and quality in service provision. This type of health care agenda relies on innovative behaviour and should rightly be thought of as an opportunity which the professionals in the NHS can take up and turn into a change process. The market, with its concept of purchaser and provider relationships, was a crude device for creating an element of vulnerability and crisis in the NHS. Given the effort and resources used to establish the market, the impact it has made on medical management is of questionable significance.

4 The medical managers

The previous chapter discussed the sense of opportunity and anxiety engendered by the need to respond to the radical terms of the 1990 NHS Act. In this chapter the post-Working for Patients organizational 'fall-out' is examined by considering the changes in medical management in the NHS trusts. While the political centre were happy to see NHS managers work sixty-hour weeks drawing up contracts, securing deals, pursuing mergers and so on, the chaos had to stop before it reached the primary figures responsible for allocating resources and delivering care at operational level – the doctors. Medical directors and clinical directorates were the initial organizational device used to absorb the shock of the Working for Patients induced changes. In a sense it can be claimed that clinical directors are the feature of the post-Working for Patients that have sustained the previous tradition of management by remote control. On the other hand, clinical directors are to some the beginning of an exciting phase in medical management.

The radicalism of Working for Patients was counterbalanced by the lack of progress made with the development of the resource management initiative and medical audit as the basis of a management control system. The market arrived without there being a means for managers to control the resource consuming behaviour of the medical profession. The 'chaos of the market' was represented in Working for Patients as a new era of competition and choice, where no longer could steady lines of patients be guaranteed to come through a hospital's clinics and wards. The shock of market forces was supposed to cause a once and for all shift in the *frontier of control* as trust managers struggled to cost out treatments and secure the quality and prices buyers of services demanded in the internal market (Harrison 1994). Given the clear variations that existed in doctor's use of resources the chain of managerial control had to be tightened around the medical profession, or trusts would be unable to survive in the newly competitive environment created by the 1990 NHS Act. In addition, a sense of corporate responsibility among the medical profession was surely a pre-requisite for effective strategic and operational management of NHS trusts. Both responses implied a radical change for doctors' relationship to the management process. The discussion of medical directors and clinical directorates presented below is based on the conclusion that in reality no fundamental shift has as yet taken place on an NHS-wide basis. However, at the level of the individual NHS trust or medical practice, doctors are participating in management systems which are significantly new and challenging in nature to warrant attention.

Managing hospital doctors

In the 1980s it was hoped that physicians could be incorporated in the management process through appointment to general management posts and through their participation in the then management budgeting exercise. The re-launched resource management initiative remains high up the official management agenda but in reality has slipped from view in many trusts. Management is still seen as a separate process essentially there to serve the doctors rather than utilize their abilities to influence costs and quality and make changes happen. Earlier Griffiths had failed to appreciate the extent to which senior hospital doctors' managerial competencies were located at an operational level based on the specialty or sub-specialty service their clinical teams provided. For the same reasons that had existed pre-Working for Patients, these skills were not at the disposal of trust chief executives.

Instinct and expediency in the internal market

Faced with a need to control medical resources without a management system that could secure control over clinical behaviour, the immediate solution for managers in NHS hospitals was the appointment of medical directors to the trust board and the creation of clinical directorates to manage specific services. Medical directors are, in important respects, fulfilling the same role that the public health trained chief medical officers provided on the old health authority-based hospital management structure. Clinical directorates, it can be claimed, provide a familiar and politically non-threatening means of controlling the medical profession within the new market environment. Alternatively, clinical directors may represent the first stage in a move towards decentralizing management to the operational level of health service provision – an idea central to the Griffiths Report (Ham and Hunter 1988).

With the exception of a need to appoint a doctor to sit as an executive member of the board, trust chief executives were not directed by the 1990

Act in respect of changes in medical management arrangements they would need to make to meet the demands of the internal market. Yet, following Working for Patients, an essential organizational requirement for self-managed provider units was to be in a position to tender for contracts. This in turn implied a need for discipline among clinical staff in their use of resources in delivering services to contractually bound costs and standards. It was clearly understood that consultants running clinical teams were still distant from the strategic level of decision making. With a short-term problem of some magnitude confronting them it is not surprising therefore that trust chief executives looked to existing forms of control to get them through the first hurdle of establishing contracts with health boards and fundholding general practices.

Medical directors

Two clear management positions were created for doctors in the post-Working for Patients NHS. All trusts are required to appoint a consultant to the post of 'medical director'. Along with the general manager, chief nursing officer and the director of finance, this appointee forms the executive core of the board running an NHS trust. The implications of self-governing hospitals for the role of medical director are important.

The position of medical representative pre-Working for Patients was ill defined, and in reality the role sought by the physician in the post depended on individual priorities. Examples of proactive, corporate-minded medical directors can no doubt be located in the history of a number of hospitals. However, it is correct to conclude that the old 'cogwheel' structure invented in the late 1960s did little to develop the role of medical director/chairman of the medical committee/medical representative. Medical representatives had little in the way of formal power over colleagues. They were elected by the consultants to act as eyes and ears, spokesman and occasional arbiter, rather than to construct and lead the consultants' interest in hospital management and policy making. In certain hospitals, the medical representative on the consensus management teams of the 1970s or the unit management teams of the post-Griffiths 1980s were there to help smooth the way for implementation of decisions taken by the administrators. In some cases the medical representative would see his role as preventing encroachment of administrative influence into 'medical areas'. In other hospitals the medical representative would act as a 'fixer' procuring resources for favoured colleagues. The medical representative might, in hostile medical communities, be preoccupied with resolving or keeping the lid on simmering disputes between senior consultants. The role was a product of personal priorities and local circumstances. A particular incident might shift the emphasis away from one role to another for a time. For example, a programme of ward closures initiated by an administrator or general manager might unite a previously divided medical body and change the priorities of the medical representatives. The system of linking doctors to management through the cogwheel divisions and post of medical representative was characterized by inconsistency and prone to *ad hoc* responses to 'local difficulties'. Though some powerful or ingenious individuals may have excelled in this area, little in the way of strategic leadership was actively offered or sought from the medical representative. Lugon and Mills (1994) suggest that there is still a 'continuing lack of high expectation' on the part of trust chief executives.

The appointment of medical directors to trust boards provided the first step towards an accommodation of old structures with new demands. Given the history of the NHS it is not surprising to find the 'common sense' view being expressed that medical directors sitting on trust boards are representatives of their professional colleagues (Baker 1994: 50–6). Yet this is in direct contradiction of the NHS Act 1990. Medical directors are formally part of a corporate management team to which they bring a particular knowledge of the hospitals' operational capacities. The medical directors in reality find themselves in a more ambiguous role which combines the statutory responsibility for providing medical advice, with the added responsibility of leading trust policies in the medical domain and acting as a conduit for their professional colleagues' views on the board. The blurring of medical advice and medical management roles is particularly hard to reconcile with standard concepts of line management. Defined in terms of skills the medical directors of NHS trusts require all the political and administrative talents that successful area medical officers demonstrated in the old NHS, coupled with a flair for business. In addition, most medical directors will attempt to maintain a clinical contribution, although this varies between medical directors who took up their posts on a full-time basis and those who are strictly part-time and maintain a reduced clinical load. The conflict between these roles is unresolved but perhaps intentionally so. Medical directors were not initially part of the statutory list of board members that trusts are required to appoint. The BMA treated this as a case of losing influence. It is likely that in many cases the presence of a doctor on the board is a continuation of the old health authority tradition of using the medical officer as a go between with the doctors.

The use of the medical director varies from trust to trust. Many medical directors still define their role as professional as opposed to management. Often, medical directors will have been the chair of the local medical committee and have experience of sitting on the old health authority/board. Some medical directors will be involved in contracting, others will not.

Relationships with medical colleagues and in particular clinical directors are clearly of key significance to the contribution that medical directors make to the management process. Open hostility is relatively rare. As one medical director said, if clinical directors disagreed with him this did not result in conflict – they would simply ignore him. Medical directors generally will be concerned to retain the goodwill of the professional body as a priority.

In some trusts medical directors will be considering a move into the chief executive post. This is, however, likely to be the exception rather than the norm. Most medical directors will retain sufficient clinical sessions so as to keep them in touch with their specialism and allow them the option of a return to full-time practice.

In Scotland the medical directors quickly formed an association and gained access to the management executive in an advisory-communications capacity. A similar association is likely to be created in England. The extent to which the leadership of the NHS in Scotland and England see medical directors as an alternative source of information and knowledge to that traditionally offered by the Royal Colleges, General Council and the BMA is unclear but potentially significant.

Clinical directorates

The clinical directorate, which has become a visible face of the new medical management, has radical origins as a concept in health care management but has come to serve a conservative purpose in the NHS of the 1990s. In the mid-1990s it is clear that the term 'clinical director' or its derivatives (see below) mean different things in different places. Yet a directorate system where a consultant has designated management and budgetary responsibilities has been almost universally adopted in the NHS trusts. The reasons for giving the redesign of medical management structure a high priority were apparent to all.

The old cogwheel system of representation (see Chapter 2) had never been seen as a part of the management chain. The cogwheel divisions were instead used and thought of in professional terms. Although never formally an NHS policy, trust managers were encouraged by representative bodies such as National Association of Health Authorities and Trusts (NAHAT) and the Institute of Health Services Management (IHSM) to adopt the organizational concept of clinical directorates as a means of linking corporate management to clinical activity. As in many other areas of the health care reforms, the centre failed to specify the form that the sub-unit organizational structure was to take. The origins of clinical directorates are to be found in responses made by doctors at the grass roots. Following the failure of a temporary closure of 100 beds at Guy's in 1984 as a means of saving money, a group of clinicians began to take an interest in identifying a more systematic method of operational management at specialty level. The outcome was an agreement to experiment with the 'Johns Hopkins' model of medical management based on department sub-units called clinical directorates (Chantler 1993). The clinical directorates model began to gain ascendancy as the basic model, the lead given by the doctors who involved themselves in the official and unofficial resource management pilot sites. The BMA, IHSM and the Royal College of Physicians have all subsequently given approval to the clinical directorates model in the form of guidelines for implementation (BMA 1990; Harwood and Boufford 1993; Hopkins 1993; Disken *et al.* 1990). The IHSM version of clinical directorates has become the standard model for hospitals adopting this system of organization. Capewell (1992: 441–7) has observed that in Scotland the tendency is for hospitals to operate with a structure that includes a unit general manager, a unit management team, a clinical services coordinator and a unit medical manager who will chair a clinical directors' committee, which includes all clinical directors and directors of services such as laboratories. There will be perhaps six directorates in a small trust and as many as sixteen in a large teaching hospital. Capewell believes there ought to be between three and ten consultants in each clinical directorate. If there are too few it is difficult to justify management time and if there are too many there will be differences in clinical activities practised by sub-specialties.

Clinical directorates have most frequently been created around the six or so main medical areas:

- medicine
- surgery
- O and G plus paediatrics
- paediatrics plus O and G
- orthopaedics and trauma
- Anaesthesia (plus ITUs and theatres).

(This is the model advocated by the IHSM.)

Less frequently the doctors are organized on the basis of a much longer list of specialties, sub-specialties and clinical services. This is sometimes referred to as the 'Leicester model' (Barker 1990):

1 surgery and specialties
2 ENT and ophthalmology
3 medicine and specialties
4 ITU and CCU
5 A and E and orthopaedics
6 paediatric medicine and surgery
7 O and G and community midwifery
8 anaesthesia and theatres
9 clinical laboratories
10 radiology and medical physics
11 pharmacy and therapy services
12 commercial services
13 general services
14 nursing
15 estates
16 finance
17 information
18 personnel.

Selection, post titles and careers

The implications of trust chief executives appointing a colleague to 'direct' them was not received well by the doctors in some trusts. Accordingly, the clinicians heading up recognizably similar medical groupings may be known as Specialty Coordinator, Clinical Coordinator or occasionally Clinical Manager. The selection process whereby clinical directors were appointed was carried out in a fashion typical to a medical organization but inexplicable outside this special context. Capewell likened their selection to the process whereby old Tory leaders used to 'emerge'. Sometimes the chairman of the old cogwheel division have simply been redesignated as clinical directors. In other situations, however, the clinical directors seem to have been 'acclaimed' by their colleagues. There is also evidence to suggest that postholders came forward rather reluctantly in some cases. The clinician selected had to be acceptable to as many of their professional colleagues as possible and appear to be someone who could handle management tasks competently.

Reconciling control over the finance, quantity and quality of patient services in the office of the clinical director is a rational managerial solution but is reliant on the acquiescence of consultants. While it was possible to use the vocabulary of management in drawing up job specifications, the selection process in the first round of appointments which took place in 1992 in most trusts was influenced by the recognized tension between management and professional responsibilities. Clinical directors in some places will quite definitely be seen as having 'done the decent thing' and come forward to take on a role that would keep managers out of the specialty level of operations in the trusts. In other places a 'press gang' attitude will have been evident. Most clinical directors will continue to spend substantial parts of their time in clinical work. Often an incentive has existed for specialty groupings in the form of over-compensation for the loss of the clinical directors' clinical contribution. Sometimes a clinical directors' 'management time' will be 'paid' back in the form of a generously funded new appointment at an appropriate level. Such deals have thus perpetuated the tradition of specialties bargaining with management for more resources, in the new circumstance of clinical directorates.

For consultants, the traditional route to the pinnacle of the professional ladder has involved taking part in 'medical politics' – the local medical advisory committee, the Royal Colleges, the BMA, working on the General Medical Council – and 'finished' with formal academic achievements. In certain teaching hospitals appointment to the post of clinical director is not seen as reaching the peak of a local hierarchy, although it may prove to be a significant stage in a consultant's career progress.

Clinical directors almost always took up their appointments on a part-time basis. A sharp disincentive existed against taking up posts on a full-time basis if consultants were at a stage of their careers where continued progress in their clinical field was required in order to achieve a merit award. Typically, payment is being made to clinical directors on a calculation involving a certain number of sessions. The financial reward for becoming a clinical director is in itself not enough to convince doctors to step into medical management roles. However, it is worth speculating as to whether the recent introduction of a revised set of guidelines for awarding merit pay to consultants, will have major consequences in promoting the importance of medical management as a career stage for doctors. While the Advisory Committee on Discretionary Awards remains dominated by the Royal Colleges' nominees, there is now a minority NHS management membership which includes the Chief Executive of the NHS Executive and representatives of the trusts and purchasers along with representatives from Scotland and Wales. The Kendell Report was implemented during 1995, allowing for considerably greater employer (trust board) input to be made into the process whereby the Advisory Committee on Discretionary Awards allocate discretionary points to consultants (NHS Executive 1995a). (Discretionary points replaced the former C award element in the consultant's pay structure.)

In addition, the NHS Executive signalled in 1995 that the trusts ought to have more influence on the award of the more valuable distinction awards made to consultants. (The A and B distinction awards for outstanding professional contribution to the NHS (NHS Executive 1995b).) As of April 1996, consultants' contracts will either be held by the individual trusts or the NHS Executive Regional Offices (England). Potentially, chief executives have a mechanism for influencing consultants through the ability to reward. From 1995, trusts joined the list of bodies allowed to nominate consultants for discretionary awards. Outstanding management effort including the implementation of innovations became one of the seven criteria to be used in deciding who is given a discretionary award. The executive letter also specifically refers to the eligibility of part-time medical directors and clinical directors whose management contribution will be taken into account by the Advisory Committee on Discretionary Awards along with their clinical work.

For those consultants with discretionary awards moving into medical director and clinical director posts on a full-time basis, protection of the monetary value of the award became a subject for negotiation with the trust board. Against this, a counter-incentive exists in the form of the explicit and more immediate financial gain to be made from private practice. Private practice has gradually become a lucrative source of income for a larger proportion of the consultant body over the last decade. Although it is too early to say for certain, it is unlikely that doctors who are developing a large private practice will be attracted to the demands of the medical manager's role.

Clinical directors – what should they be doing?

With clinical directorates having been established in virtually all the NHS trusts by the early 1990s the BMA–IHSM – British Association of Medical

Managers (BAMM) – Royal College of Nursing (RCN) jointly authored a report providing a consensus statement on what is thought to work in clinical management. (BAMM is the British Association of Medical Managers, formed to represent the new category of doctors with a contractually specified management responsibility) (Harwood and Boufford 1993). The report identifies clinical directors with a principle role of coordinating and developing patient services. Clinical directors should have managerial control over nursing and paramedic staff. In their duties they should be supported by a nurse manager and business manager with appropriate administrative and clerical staff attached to the directorate. The business managers, it says, should be concentrating on administration, information technology, budgeting, planning, records, staff, medical secretaries and sometimes porters and cleaners. In larger directorates there is a case for employing an information manager, an accountant and resource management officer. Smaller directorates, on the other hand, may share a business manager, or appoint someone on a lower point on the pay scale or alternately combine the roles of nurse manager and business manager. (The report also notes that occasionally nurses have been appointed to the post of clinical director.) A clear problem is believed to exist where clinical directors are having to learn to carry out functional management roles such as accountancy or routine administrative tasks. By the mid-1990s many trusts who had initially begun with a large number of directorates were considering reducing the numbers in an effort to provide an appropriate level of administrative support.

Attempts are quite frequently made to prescribe the key responsibilities which clinical directors ought to be acquiring. A good example is the list compiled by Stuart and Hicks (1993: 2–5):

1 Strategic planning and implementing change (binding consultants to statement of intent and clarifying individual requirements under strategy).
2 Clinical directors need to establish a small number of standing committees (e.g. safety) and be responsible for organizing work through task forces.
3 Communications – the clinical director should assume responsibility for ensuring an effective system operates.
4 Clinical directors should create protocols and policies to replace folklore – managing 'how you learn' in the clinical directorate.
5 Time management – clinical director needs to create free time.
6 Keeping files.
7 Delegating tasks and performance appraisal.
8 Clinical budgets – controlling operations – establishing a role for a dedicated business manager on site in contact with members of the directorate to heighten fiscal responsibility.

In truth, if the Stuart and Hicks list is taken as a reasonable indication of the clinical director's functional responsibilities, then an examination of the diaries of a cross-section of clinical directors is likely to reveal highly varied apportioning of time to each of the categories of activity. Mahmood and Chisnell's (1993) survey of consultants in the Wirral NHS Trust indicated that there were about forty different management subjects identified as being of some importance to them. The extent to which clinical directors can be termed managers is questionable. The balance between the 'idealized' management tasks – a mix of planning, setting objectives, leading, motivating and the aspects of the clinical director's role which is uniquely concerned with coordinating the specialty is unclear, apparently varying from trust to trust and even clinical director to clinical director within trusts. Huxham and Botham (1995) refer to the different orientations of medical managers to the 'small m' and 'big M' managerial tasks. Some clinical directors and medical directors will be attracted to the 'big M' role of strategy former and leader, while others will see their role in inter-professional terms emphasizing the 'small m' tasks traditionally expected of senior doctors. Fitzgerald (1992) argues that the part-time status of clinical directors and the fact that they are highly trained professionals means that the role played by clinicians in the management process should 'use or adapt to the high level of skills and clinical knowledge'. This is a strongly held view among many clinicians but equally many clinical directors will wish to develop new management skills and this is reflected in the large numbers undertaking MBAs and other courses offered by universities. Mark (1991) sees the latter development in a positive light, pointing out the likelihood that clinicians interested in a management role will be attracted to the possibilities of learning to manage in the familiar context of their own specialty.

Clinical directorates and accountability

Much of the variation in how clinical directors allocate their time and efforts is to be explained by different types of accountability and professional relationships encountered in the trusts. Clinical directors are appointees of the trust chief executive. Formally, clinical directors are part of a line management structure, they report to the chief executive and are responsible to the board of the trust. Actual accountability, on the other hand, is complex. In many trusts the clinical directors will perceive themselves as being part of a line management structure where the medical director is their immediate boss. In other trusts this is not the case.

If clinical directors have 'delegated authority' from their chief executive, they also remain, in an immediate sense, professionally accountable to their patients, their fellow doctors on a collegiate basis, and more formally through offices of a trust medical advisory committee where these still exist. There may also be a 'division' or committee which draws together consultants in particular specialties. Additionally, accountability to their Royal College, the General Medical Council and the local health authority/board through the chief medical officer are features of the clinical director's life. The doctors who work within the directorate are tied into exactly the same sets of accountability, further complicating lines of authority. The nurse manager, too, may be involved in similarly complex accountability relationships with the Royal College of Nursing and the trust's chief nursing officer where this post still exists. As stated above, the selection process typically undertaken by trusts did not necessarily produce a situation where clinical directors were likely to secure a happy marriage of popularity, seniority and professional prestige with which to ally to the formal positional authority of the post. The accountability issue is complex with clinical directors being seen as 'authority' figures in a limited sense and perhaps for the most part confined to areas that do not impinge on clinical practice.

Precisely how clinical directors are supposed to relate to their clinical colleagues is a matter for negotiation between the interested parties at specialty level. The general structure of relationships are reasonably easy to identify with directorates covering a discernible self-contained clinical grouping, for example, orthopaedic surgery or radiology. It is those enduring profession-based structures, ties and responsibilities that are hard to characterize in any systematic fashion. In one teaching hospital recently examined a deliberate bid has been made to separate responsibilities. Clinical directors may attend the medical advisory committee as full members but they will be barred from chairing that committee (BMA 1990). A clinical directors committee will probably meet on a regular basis to resolve management issues. The same committee may well be expected to 'keep off' the locally accepted territory of the medical advisory committee.

There are signs in the mid-1990s that the clinical directorate is becoming the main focus for medical matters, but this is to ignore very significant numbers of trusts where earlier forms of medical representation are still dominant.

Managing a directorate

From a rational or perhaps naive perspective it is clear that clinical directors ought to be key figures in the internal market, providing the link between the trust board and operational performance (Iles *et al.* 1993: 179–85). As head of 'operational units' the clinical director would be assumed to be the person best placed to manage the performance of clinical staff in line with corporate objectives. This is a role which few clinical directors have attempted to play. In general terms, the creation of clinical directors has not been used to close down clinical autonomy. The selection criteria did not result in the appointment of a new breed of doctors with a clear aim of controlling clinical behaviour. As explained above, the doctors who came forward to act as clinical directors were generally not driven by a desire to take the management torch into uncharted clinical waters. The clinical director typically sits in a negotiated order where sensitivity to the power wielded by colleagues will tend to cause the cautious to draw back from managing clinical activity on a one-to-one basis. This being the case, it is nevertheless true that many clinical directors will be successful in wielding influence through gentle exhortation or education. For example, colleagues may be encouraged to compare their prescribing patterns with one another with consequent changes in behaviour. Whether this is 'management' proper is a matter for debate. Within directorates a spectrum would appear to exist between a hierarchical model where, within an understood field of competence, the clinical director will act as a chief officer and the Guy's/Johns Hopkins model which rests on the 'clinical management team' as a type of consensus management bringing together both clinical and managerial disciplines (Sims and Sims 1993).

The power problem apart, it will be unusual for clinical directors to have at their disposal a resource management system capable of giving them the information they require to manage doctors' behaviour in any detailed sense. The introduction of clinical directorates ran parallel with the 'roll-out' of the resource management initiative. The resource management initiative was intended to place resource consuming decisions at the level at which best judgement could be exercised – an important idea in the Griffiths Report. In the event this has tended to mean the office of the clinical director rather than individual clinicians. The resource management initiative as envisaged in the Griffiths Report was to take decision making down to the level of the individual consultant. In reality the resource management initiative (or its watered-down cousins) tended to be absorbed into the clinical directorate management process. It is not surprising that the resource management initiative found its home at this level. Given the implications inherent in the resource management initiative process for clinical freedom the objectives usually had to be camouflaged. Often the resource management initiative was sold as an educational or research tool which individual clinicians might use for their own interest.

Clinical directors, in the absence of a management system for effectively controlling clinical behaviour, may be providing a convenient means of extending traditional resource capping control a little further down the organization and as members of the profession also effectively keeping managers at bay. Although clinical directors are nominally responsible for a budget it has to be accepted that in many cases the pattern of expenditure remains beyond their control, owing its form to the aggregated decisions made by individual clinicians. The ability of clinical directors to add a new dimension to health service management is not yet clear. If, for example, a trust is faced with a serious budget deficit will the clinical directors be both willing and in a position to carry out a re-configuration of the service provision in a fashion not previously achievable in terms of sophistication of judgement and action?

Also of great potential significance is the extent to which clinical directors are involved in the contracting process. This varies from situations where clinical directors are leading negotiations supported by other staff to the opposite extreme where clinical directors are not involved at all. Where clinical directors are closely involved in the contracting process they can be in a uniquely strong position to re-configure services in response to needs expressed by purchasing authorities and fundholding GPs. The clinical director is likely to be the person most able to understand what purchasers require and in turn make an assessment as to what the directorate sees as a reasonable and achievable response. For example, a clinical director can decide to do more day cases on the basis of his or her knowledge of colleagues' clinical abilities and orientations in a way that a non-medical business manager cannot.

Greatorex and Edgell (1993) argue that clinical directors should be influencing purchasers through their command of local intelligence and their ability to promote the boards' interpretation of national and local priorities. The clinical director should also be undertaking health needs assessments and be reconciling these with financial constraints. This is a type of strategic shaping of health care provision. There is also a marketing role to be played, identifying customers, customer wants and responding, making sure that customers are kept informed of changes made. Fulfilment of such a contribution is dependent on the ability to use information systems effectively. A third role in the contracting process should be constructed around a quality improvement strategy. In this scheme the clinical director is in effect playing a leading role in health care strategy by using his or her special position and knowledge of resource inputs, the clinical process, patient turnover, waiting times, health care outputs and outcomes (quality of life and satisfaction) to influence customer's interpretation of health needs. Were clinical directors to succeed in this role a significant contribution would be made to remove the split between primary and secondary care in the UK.

The making of medical managers

The study made of clinical directors and medical directors by Mole and Dawson (1993) provides a useful record of medical managers' experiences in the NHS of the 1990s. Medical managers are concerned to balance their management role with the need to continue with clinical practice for reasons of professional credibility and also long-term financial opportunities. The medical managers surveyed expressed a concern over the ease by which successors could be identified. Regarding the actual management tasks associated with their posts, a clear difficulty is recognized in respect of managing and directing their colleagues. As indicated elsewhere clinical directors and medical directors are not vested with line management type authority. Influence has to be bargained. Some medical managers will find this a hard fact to reconcile themselves to. On a more specific subject, medical managers are often dissatisfied with the level of control they have over budgets, while at the same time feeling pressurized to meet corporate requirements. The extent to which personnel issues have been moved into clinical directorates varies, but clinical directors seemed to regard the flexibility afforded by devolved control over staff as a worthwhile gain.

Clinical directors' depth of involvement with contracting is another area where the survey revealed considerable variations. In some trusts the clinical directors are required to re-configure service patterns in response to the feedback they get from taking part in negotiations. In many other situations clinical directors have little direct involvement with negotiating the patterns of services to be provided. The study also identified a feeling among medical managers that they must undertake specialist management training if they were to be successful. Human resources, financial management, information management, marketing and business management are all types of functional management which medical managers must be expected to oversee or take part in. A familiar route for clinical directors involves taking some management training either in the form of an MBA or other management higher degree, or alternatively taking short courses run by universities on aspects of medical management.

An opportunity cost exists in taking on a medical director's job or becoming a clinical director. According to Frostick and Wallace (1993: 245-6) the pay-offs are to be found in the satisfaction of running something akin to your own business, creating a better work environment, assuming greater responsibility and influence over the use of resources. A lightened clinical load and a financial incentive represent more tangible rewards. By the end of the 1990s with many medical managers having invested in management training of a formal or 'on the job' type it will be easier to see if management has emerged as a career option for doctors in the NHS.

Are clinical directorates working?

A certain degree of justifiable optimism has been attached to the development of clinical directorates. For some commentators clinical directorships represented an alternative means of bringing doctors into management to that offered by the resource management initiative (RMI). Mark (1991) saw medical managers as key figures in making doctors more responsible in their use of resources, reducing the conflict between 'centre' and 'periphery' and as a means of conveying an impression of making a concession to the doctors in return for their loss of input to hospital management through the former 'tripartite' structure of the pre-Griffiths consensus management era.

For Capewell (1992) the case for clinical directors is to be expressed in terms of bringing management closer to physical resources (theatres laboratories, out-patients departments or specialty groupings), enhanced teamwork in specialty groups, improved organizational flexibility to cope with new technology, political changes and financial constraints.

Evidence can be found without much difficulty which shows clinical directors and medical directors making advances in precisely these terms. Yet equally a suspicion certainly exists as to the extent to which medical directors and clinical directors provide a convenient means for government and trust managers to pass over responsibility for unpopular health policies (Health Service Journal 1993). Clinical directors recorded their dissatisfaction with the internal market which they claimed was failing to ensure that money followed patients. The prospect of endlessly delivering cost-improvements in order to carry out more work for less money was not attractive (Kingman 1993).

Participation in management by doctors must be seen to produce tangible benefits as medical directors and clinical directors influence local health services provision in a strategic manner. This is dependent on the extent to which a management relationship has been forged between the clinical directors and their professional colleagues in respect of clinical practice. Advances in this aspect of managing clinical directorates are variable but with clear indications available that clinical autonomy is still largely intact. The tools for managing clinical practice for greater efficiency and effectiveness are developing, but it will be a rare case where a clinical director is using an audit system to identify underperforming colleagues and subsequently act upon this evidence.

The means of controlling the operational performance of hospital doctors have advanced somewhat since the introduction of general management in the 1980s. Nevertheless, the Griffiths-inspired drive to push resource-consuming decisions down to the level where they could be best made is far from complete. A traditional centralized style of management has been used to make the internal market work. This form of control remains constrained in its influence over clinical behaviour. At worst, medical directors and clinical directors will be used as go-betweens in a familiar book-balancing exercise that involves closing wards periodically, not filling vacancies and cancelling operations. At best they are the basis for a new strategically led style of corporate management in the NHS. Much will depend on the medical managers identifying a career pathway out of the aftermath of the 1990s reforms.

5 Doctors and performance management in the National Health Service

The previous chapter examined the recent developments in medical management and in particular the creation of the posts of medical director and clinical director. It was made clear that medical managers are not (as yet) assuming a typical line management role in relation to the management of their colleagues' performance. The manner in which clinical directors are appointed makes it unlikely that such a position could readily be adopted by most. With this predicament in mind this chapter deals with the 'technologies of control' – the tools for monitoring and changing the behaviour of doctors. From a decidedly 'low-tech' status at the beginning of the 1980s, the work of researchers has led to performance measurement systems becoming more sophisticated over the last fifteen years. The performance management systems reviewed below must be considered in the context of medical management as discussed previously. However, technical excellence in design in no way guarantees that a technology will be utilized to any great effect in the NHS, given the weakness of both medical and non-medical managers in relation to doctors at operational levels. Nevertheless, the rapidly developing systems for measuring performance are increasingly recognized as a threat to medical autonomy in the UK and elsewhere.

A considerable range of devices are currently being used to measure and potentially begin to control doctors' performance. Understanding the origins of performance management is an important step in conducting an appraisal of the potential impact that technologies of control can make in the context of the management of doctors in the NHS. The difficulties in implementing a programme of performance evaluation are examined with consideration given to the health service's 'stakeholder's dilemma'. Technologies of control are also to be considered in relation to whether a scheme is originated and operated by the medical profession or by 'external managers' – an important factor in assessing potential impacts. There is also the question of the level at which clinical performance management is conducted – whether it is the hospital, specialty, family medical practice or the individual clinician that is the 'accounting unit'. At this relatively early stage in the development of medical management in the NHS, the conceptual basis and methods for measuring and controlling performance should constantly be scrutinized. Particular attention should be directed at off-the-peg 'systems' like total quality management which attracted interest in the 1990s. Consumer pressure may yet prove to be the single most important factor in re-stating the autonomy of doctors from performance management. The growth of consumerism in relation to health care is discussed accordingly. A brief examination of the impact of consumer satisfaction measurement on the behaviour of doctors working for health maintenance organizations (HMOs) in the United States, is conducted.

The politics of performance management

First, a brief overview of the political context of management technologies in the NHS. In the not-for-profit NHS, performance should be measured against contribution made to government policy on health care. Yet there is only a fairly recent tradition of attempting to evaluate policies in the public sector, let alone the contribution of individual hospitals or doctors. The tradition of public accountability, which goes back to the mid-nineteenth century, stresses legality and regularity, with a clear emphasis on economy not outcomes (Drewry and Butcher 1988: 39–45). This is an obvious bias in public sector management and partly explains the inclination to experiment with market mechanisms for allocating resources effectively. Certainly, prior to the Griffiths report, management accounting information systems in the NHS were dominated by financial reporting for purposes of public accountability and the need to exert control over global budgets. NHS management had traditionally been led by the public expenditure process in central government and translated into a hierarchical budget allocation process by NHS administrators in the regions and localities. The doctors, in retrospect, were largely unaware of management, which was something that went on somewhere else in the hierarchy. Little attention was paid to medical performance management.

Since the 1980s, management technologies of control can be understood as being intended to influence the behaviour of doctors with respect to the efficiency, economy and effectiveness of service delivery – the three Es of performance management (Carter 1991). Implementation balance between the three Es has been uneven. Initially, economy was stressed. The policy device of cash limits imposed on public sectors bodies from 1976 onwards meant that resources did not follow activity, instead activity had to be funded to a level consistent with a fixed budget. This was still a form of arms' length control based on a concept of economy familiar to the NHS but much tougher for managers to work under (Gray and Jenkins 1985:

104–6). A concern to make the public sector efficiency conscious was given a symbolic political emphasis by the Prime Minister Margaret Thatcher when she backed the establishment of the Cabinet Office Efficiency Unit under Derek Rayner in 1979. Rayner (later Sir Derek) was a senior executive with Marks and Spencers. Fittingly, given the focus on management not policy, he had neither a civil service nor academic background. The Efficiency Unit had a very narrow remit under him. 'Rayner scrutinies' as they were known examined bread and butter value for money issues, initially in the civil service itself, but later replicated in other public sector bodies. (The term 'bread and butter' can be applied literally since the scrutinies were in some instances pitched at the level of analysing the costs that were incurred in making sandwiches for civil service canteens.) Kellener (1980) described the Rayner approach as like focusing a laser beam on the managerial effectiveness of activities that supported existing policies rather than using an arc lamp to illuminate the broader ground and ask why a policy was carried out in the first place. The Efficiency Unit was to be judged in terms of its ability in rooting out the most efficient way of getting from A to B. These types of 'value-for-money' studies stay off the policy makers turf. There is no opportunity to question whether it is actually desirable to get to position B in the first place. In simple terms, an 'X-efficiency'-based calculation was being made of inputs over outputs. If an agency or public sector institution can reduce resource inputs and maintain the same output then an efficiency gain is made. A gain is also made when output is increased with the same level of resource inputs maintained (Glynn 1992: 1–12).

The Efficiency Unit carried out its first studies in the NHS during 1982. The unit's performance auditors were seen as short-term 'shock troopers' (Drewry and Butcher 1988). Their contribution to public accountability was acknowledged in the Financial Management Initiative of 1982 which extended efficiency-orientated financial delegation throughout Whitehall in the spirit of efficiency unit investigations (Gray and Jenkins 1991: 45–9). Additionally, the first set of DHSS performance indicators were produced in 1983 with which regional health authorities and district health authorities were asked to compare their performance against national and regional norms. The Rayner scrutinies more generally served to legitimate a particular type of efficiency investigation. Value-for-money methodology was rolled out specifically through the work of the Audit Commission in local government and after 1990 in the NHS. Initially, the impact of efficiency audit was constrained by the concentration on the resource inputs side of the calculation. The reasons will be clear in relation to health care where it is often extremely difficult to establish robust output measures. For instance, suspicions were rife by the late 1980s that 'revolving door' discharge-admission policies were being employed in some parts of the NHS. Such practices which allowed patients to be double-counted as 'through-puts' were being encouraged by district health authorities because of how their hospital units looked against the efficiency indicators. While perhaps a degree of connivance in such efficiency 'scams' could be wrought out of groups of clinicians, for the most part the medical profession, collectively and individually, remained aloof (Harrison *et al.* 1992: 104–9). Without medical cooperation in the process of setting professional standards at Royal College level, management by efficiency is destined to remain on the fringes of clinical activity. No signs of interest have been made by the leaders of the medical professions regarding the endorsement of efficiency concepts.

An evaluation-led health service?

The enthusiasm for efficiency and economy indicators has waned in the 1990s. In contrast, considerable professional interest now centres on the concept 'health gain', which is the NHS's answer to industry's concept of 'added value' and implies that each contribution or sequence of activities in health care processes are subjected to a critical examination as to what they actually contribute to the whole intervention. Sir Roy Griffiths had in 1983 been concerned by the lack of precision in objective setting in the NHS. He laid the blame squarely on the absence of systematic evaluation of outcome effectiveness:

> ... there is little measurement of health output; clinical evaluation of particular practices is by no means common and economic evaluation extremely rare. Nor can the NHS display a ready assessment of the effectiveness with which it is meeting the needs and expectations of the people it serves.
>
> (NHS Management Inquiry 1983)

On the face of it, measures of effectiveness have a more immediate resonance with the traditions of professional leadership and regulation in the NHS. Outcome effectiveness can be said to be conditioned by the extent to which clinical practices deliver outputs that match desired results and therefore, if measured convincingly, provide a sound basis for managing doctors' behaviour. The Royal Colleges are primarily concerned with regulating and developing clinical practice and might therefore be thought of as natural allies in outcome-led policy evaluation. On a scientific level, 'evidence based' practice is developing through investigations into particular procedures such as the treatment of 'glue-ear' or hysterectomies (Sheldon 1994). Yet in practice it will prove difficult to match health policies, management practice, professional regulation of clinical practice and actual clinical behaviour together in a consensus over what constitutes effective health care. Measuring the effectiveness of outcomes in health care is dependent on agreement over 'values' – judgements made by parties of a health care activity as to its worth.

In the NHS, health care activities often involve a large number of professionals with widely differentiated perspectives on health care activities. Reviewing a series of definitions of effectiveness made by organizations such as the Audit Commission and Price Waterhouse, Glynn *et al.* (1992) conclude that effectiveness is a value placed on the relationship between an activity and its effect. In the NHS, values are informed by prevailing political, social and professional norms. The NHS has had to move off from a standing start in relation to evaluation. In spite of certain clinical specialties having a long history of carrying out evaluations, professions generally do not rely on formal systematic procedures for maintaining standards and identifying the usefulness of new innovations. Evaluation is time consuming and costly and unless the evaluators are trusted to get it right, no-one reacts to their findings. Getting it right is not just about using the right tools in an accurate manner. Health care outcomes are notoriously difficult to measure. It would be wrong to place too much emphasis on the scientific or procedural research basis of the evaluation process. Clearly, methodological practice is very important – evaluations are underwritten by the rigour of procedures used – but also important is the political and organizational context in which the tools are used.

Any movement towards an evaluation-led health care system must contend with the reality of measuring effectiveness, not against clearly stated and accepted policy objectives, but against a series of stakeholder values and timescales.

A well-publicized story involving Professor Michael Baum, described in the media as a breast cancer screening pioneer, is illustrative of the stakeholder problem. Baum had just resigned from the NHS advisory body on breast screening, having become convinced that the three-yearly checks on 4.5 million women in the high risk age group of 50–64 were a waste of money. He believed the checks were doing more harm than good and costing the service £27 million per year. It took £1 million to save a life according to an evaluation study referred to. Baum told the press that 'just because you were doing something efficiently it does not mean it's worthwhile'. The government, on the other hand, had been keen to link the service, which they launched in 1990, with a discernible fall in the death rate from breast cancer. So what place evaluation? The Chief Medical Officer claimed it would take another decade to see if the service did lower mortality significantly. The participants in this issue include researchers, politicians and women being screened, each group bringing different values to the calculation of the programme's effectiveness (*Sunday Times*, 3 September 1995).

Table 5.1 provides a fuller illustration of the stakeholders' perspectives on the effectiveness of clinical services. The list of stakeholders in this example comprises the politicians in government, the Department of Health/NHS Executive, trust managers, clinicians, other health professionals and patients. As a means of categorizing the differing perspectives brought to bear on the effectiveness of the clinical service the table uses concepts of 'natural habitat', 'instincts', along with 'methods for evaluating success', perceived 'payoffs' and stakeholders' 'timescales'. Indicative examples have been provided for each stakeholder. The stakeholders' natural habitats are

Table 5.1 Stakeholders in the clinical evaluation process

Stakeholders	Natural habitat	Instincts	Methods for evaluating success	Payoffs	Timescale
Politicians	Electoral	Maximize policy impact/control/publicity/minimize embarrassment	Advice from civil service/political instincts	Demonstrate leadership and gain electoral advantage	Short, determined by electoral cycle
Department of Health/NHS Executive	Bureaucratic	Control/accountability rationale of administration	Reports by professional advisers/audit agencies	As above with need to justify budgets evaluation may be an end itself	Short-medium, related to government cycles
Trust managers	Hospital	Organizational mission/organizational safety	Advice from medical director or other adviser	Opportunity to cut or expand a service	Contract lifetime
Clinicians	Hospital	Professional values/organizational safety	Current informal monitoring, peer review, research of a more formal nature	Learning professional development	Structured by career
Other health professionals	Hospital or primary care setting	As above but conditioned by specialism	As above but may have developed own specialty-based techniques	Learning professional development	Structured by career
Patients	Hospital or primary care setting in the community	Reliance on clinicians	Own experience	Health status	Lifetime

Source: Adapted from Rossi and Freeman (1989: 427–36)

the social or organizational circumstances in which they make sense of evaluations. Simple illustrations are provided in the table. While it is not possible to generalize with any degree of confidence as to stakeholders actual instincts, the example is illustrative of the type of differences that are likely to be present. Methods for evaluating success may vary between formal scientific studies conducted by clinicians, personal experience in the case of patients, performance audit conducted by a government agency, to 'reading the wind' in the case of politicians conscious of the impact on electoral popularity that health care policies have. The timescales into which evaluations of clinical services fit differ considerably. In a politically-led health service it cannot be forgotten that governments face election every five years, while Ministers face a constant threat of being moved out of office at short notice. For trust managers, the threat of being sacked shortens the timescale. Clinicians, on the other hand, are likely to see evaluation of services in longer career structured terms.

Evaluation programmes have to be designed in a manner that either identifies one stakeholder's perspective as its principal terms of reference, or finds a consensus between stakeholders with different positions (though this latter approach is less likely). According to Rossi and Freeman (1989: 441), evaluators need to develop an 'engineering tradition' which will allow them to apply principles derived from 'pure research' to real life problems. For instance, it is one thing to know that gasses expand when heated and that each gas has an expansion coefficient, but another to use this principle to manufacture economical gas turbine engines.

In the current climate, managers are expected to be able to demonstrate both 'substantive effectiveness' in delivering intended/desired effects and 'evaluative effectiveness' in the sense of being technically capable of measuring the trust's performance in delivering particular services. In other words, it is no good being able to deliver effective services if you cannot prove them to be effective. The managerial legitimacy of health services evaluation is founded on earlier attempts to measure and control economy and efficiency. Outcome evaluation has, therefore, been introduced as a process on the back of the earlier and more easily understood value for money movement which stressed economy and efficiency.

In theory, the NHS is moving towards a structure based on business units. Service evaluation ought to be a part of a system of contractual relations providing the empirical evidence for trusts or specialisms to pass market tests. However, the NHS may still be more of a hierarchy than a marketplace. Jackson (1993: 9–14) differentiates between the scientific management paradigm, which perceives evaluation in terms of control, and the strategic management perspective where evaluations are part of a learning process that is based on comparing performance against targets. For organizations like the NHS, which have been belatedly drawn into performance evaluation, this can either take the form of rating and sorting or be part of a learning process. If the NHS is based on hierarchy, then it should be understood that hierarchies have a need to allocate rewards.

Jackson believes there to be a danger that pressure from evaluation causes middle managers to feel forced to speak the language of satisfying the customer, when in reality not too much is known about the customer, and the customer is synonymous with what the boss thinks.

Doctors from their traditional standpoint outside the administrative hierarchy may, on the other hand, not see their participation in clinical evaluation as part of the management process at all. They need to be convinced of the connections between clinical standards and organizational practice. In these circumstances, there is a suspicion that evaluation will be used to serve the traditional NHS bureaucracy, with its need for references in allocating resources. Alternatively, in a world of uncertain policy objectives and hard to track health care outcomes, it can be argued that the real worth of evaluation is at the grass roots off the NHS, with practitioners working with patients to improve services rather than treating them as passive recipients. Consequently, an open dialogue may be needed where public standards are openly discussed and negotiated. It is unclear that the timeframe of the internal market, with its annual round of contracting, encourages the use of evaluation as a learning tool in medical management.

Externally owned and driven performance measurement

Chapter 3 discussed the manner with which the resource management initiative and medical audit – micro-management doctor focused technologies – were initially given high prominence in Working for Patients, but were undermined by a subsequent diminishing of political support for their use by managers in the control of doctors. Arguably, the NHS in practice still responds best to a traditional arms-length type of control exercised by government through the annual public spending allocations and through the imposition of agreed efficiency targets on health authorities. This type of performance management makes the NHS trust or the purchasing authority the accounting unit rather than clinical specialties. A distance is therefore maintained between the 'performance' being measured and doctors' operational activities.

Since the introduction of the internal market, the Efficiency Index has been used to add a degree of sophistication to the business of encouraging purchasing authorities to maximize patient activity from given resources. The Efficiency Index measures patient activity against money allocated to the following categories of health care activity:

1 ordinary admissions and day case finished consultant episodes
2 outpatient and accident and emergency attendances
3 day care attendances
4 community contacts
5 ambulance journeys.

The index relies on a heavily aggregated version of actual clinical activity, thus further extending the distance from individual doctor's performance with resources. The overall index score is constructed by adding together performance in each category weighted on the basis of size of budget. Donaldson and colleagues (1994: 3–9) argue that the index calculations also encourage spending deviations away from strategically determined priority areas such as health promotion. The index scores are used by trusts and purchasing authorities as a target, which creates an incentive for new resources to be used to improve performance against the five categories listed above. They also believe the arithmetic of the index emphasizes cost improvement in existing acute care dominated activity rather than encouraging cash releasing schemes that involve moving activity into primary and community settings. This is not a new problem or attributable to a single-performance management technology like the Efficiency Index. The bias towards incremental growth in existing budgets is well understood in organizational life generally (Ham and Hill 1984: 79–83). It should be understood, however, that the continued reliance on the Efficiency Index macro-management style of performance management using highly aggregated data does nothing to close the gap between strategy and clinical performance.

Still in the tradition of arm's length control, though with more direct linkage to doctor's performance, the league tables produced by the Department of Health use the specialty as the accounting unit. The league tables, which make it possible to compare hospital departments with one another, have been produced annually since 1994. According to Sir Duncan Nichol, then chief executive of the NHS, the tables were being produced to give the patients greater ability to 'judge, influence and choose' health services (British Medical Journal 1993). Initially, the Patient's Charter (see below, p. 72) standards included in-patient and out-patient waiting times, average waiting time in accident and emergency, the proportion of cancelled operations, the proportion of procedures performed as day cases and ambulance response times. The intention is to improve the league tables by including clinical indicators such as cross-infection rates and readmission rates. The political attention on waiting times which the league tables nevertheless inevitably attracted, has caused discomfort in some quarters. MacAlister (1994: 440–1) feared that as a result of the priority given to waiting times, some patients with painful conditions might have to wait longer for treatment because patients with minor conditions may be moved up the list of priorities to reduce waiting times in selected areas. Similarly, patients may be seen by a nurse within five minutes of arrival in an accident and emergency department, but may still face a wait of several hours before being treated.

Strategically, the league tables are potentially useful in sharpening up the environment surrounding medical management. First, in spite of what the media would tell their readers, the league tables do encompass a range of indicators and not just the politically high profile, but not necessarily all-important waiting times. Secondly, if the public take poor performance to be an indication of the state of a trust's management of clinical services, some of the blame might be attached to the doctors. GPs aware of their patient's attention to league tables could also respond to poor performances by shifting their referrals to alternative providers. This interpretation presupposes much about the behaviour of doctors. The reluctance of GPs to act like consumers, weighing up a provider's performance, has been examined in Chapter 3 and the symbiotic relationships between GPs and specialists are likely to undermine the extent to which the league tables create a harsher environment for doctors in the trusts. Also of significance is the extent to which doctors in the trusts react to the publication of performance measurements relating to their work. While medical managers described in Chapter 4 are likely to be stung by poor results, individual consultants may be indifferent. Their reactions may also be tempered by the level of aggregation or lack of a clear professional sense of engagement with the indicators as used in the tables. Progress with the development of appropriate clinical indicators is clearly important in this respect. It is not altogether apparent that doctors share a strong sense of corporate pride based on employment in a particular hospital trust. Doctors, rather like academics, may well see the hospital as a more or less congenial place for them to practice rather than as a conventional employer.

Research suggests it is far from apparent that performance indicators are of great use to general managers in relation to the control of doctors in the NHS trusts (Roberts 1990). In the 1980s the number of indicators seemed to be increasing exponentially with no-one quite sure what they really signified. At one point in the late 1980s they reached into thousands, though this had been selectively pruned back to a more digestible four hundred by 1994. Department of Health performance data is not particularly useful to the doctors in medical director or clinical director posts. Managers tended to refer to indicators haphazardly, when they could be used to support an argument.

To date, clinical outcome indicators have only been used to stimulate debate. When the Department of Health's current range of performance indicators are considered, doctors may be inclined towards the view that the design and methodological basis of hospital performance comparison is insufficiently robust. Certainly there is doubt about the validity of making comparisons between hospitals without compensating for factors such as relative deprivation. According to the Labour MP Tessa Jowell, responding to the Department of Health's removal of the social index from their data:

The length of time people stay in hospital and the degree of illness that is treated by inner-London hospitals is so heavily connected to deprivation and the social conditions in which people live that, frankly, any indicators produced without them are not worth the paper they are written on.

(Crail 1994: 10–11)

Ignoring such caution the West Midlands Regional Health Authority took a decision to publish league tables in the local press providing consultant-by-consultant breakdown of in-patient waiting times and numbers of operations performed over a year (Health Service Journal 1993). More typical is the Scottish Home and Health Department's Clinical Resource Audit Group (CRAG) publication of information describing the performance of health boards and hospitals in relation to seventeen clinical outcome indicators covering the period 1990–93. Tables were published with the stated aims of helping to raise overall standards of care and stimulating discussion about the possible reasons for any apparent variation so that appropriate action could be taken. A qualifying statement announced that, unlike the information provided in the Patient's Charter, *Raising the Standards in Scotland*, this set of indicators could not be utilized for a comparison of particular services in different hospitals. The Department saw fit to declare that differences in clinical outcome were just as likely to be attributable to differences in the characteristics of patients themselves as they were to differences in the quality and effectiveness of the treatment they received (National Health Service in Scotland, 1994b). A complex system of weighting is necessary for true comparisons to be made between, for example, mortality rates. Attention must also be given to the statistical validity of sample sizes where services are compared.

A new set of clinical outcome indicators may yet prove to be a useful tool in the hands of NHS managers in their relations with the medical profession. Øvretveit (1992) defines 'outcome' in this context as the end result of a service's interaction with a customer or population in the short-, medium- and long-term. Routine outcome measures are being developed through research programmes. For the case of in-patient treatment, routine outcome standards and measures might include emergency readmission within two weeks of discharge, post-operative infection rates, return to operating theatre for same condition and mortality and morbidity rates.

Even when performance comparisons are based on accurate data gathered according to established statistical principles and interpreted correctly, allowing for deprivation, social conditions and demographic factors, league tables will still remain talking points unless managers are empowered to examine the causes of poor results. Simple exhortation to review practices is not enough, especially since it must be acknowledged that even if doctors in departments singled out for criticism are concerned to respond for a number of reasons they may not be in a position to do anything about their performance.

A good example of the type of analysis required when poor performances are discovered is provided by the Audit Commission's (1995: 23) report on the working practices of hospital doctors – *The Doctors Tale*. The investigators were confident that failures to meet demand for specific services could be remedied by changes in procedures. They discovered that in the hospitals they examined by tradition the individual patients are referred personally to consultants by GPs or by other consultants. The relative size of consultants' caseloads are affected by the number of referrals they receive. Since the referral process is not managed, this can result in significant differences in workload between consultants. This causes difficulties in deploying doctors of all grades to meet demand efficiently. Also most hospitals' schedules for out-patient and operating theatre sessions have built up 'incrementally over the years' without the overall implications for medical staffing being reviewed. The Audit Commission claim that there is evidence that a third of general surgical and orthopaedic operations carried out as emergencies at night could be delayed until the next day if operating theatre capacity were available. The investigators found that few hospitals had rationalized the generally 'piecemeal approach' to the use of operating theatres for emergencies, 'for example, by grouping them into daily scheduled sessions'. It is questionable whether the will or capacity exists for non-medical managers to conduct inquiries such as that reported in *The Doctors' Tale* in response to a specialty's poor performance in relation to outcome indicators.

Gill (1993) has pointed out that managers will deal with, for valid reasons, a list that will include the external financial auditor, possibly the Audit Commission, the internal financial auditor, the clinical auditor, internal quality assurance teams and the purchasing authority quality assurance team. The auditors, she argues, need themselves to be audited for the effectiveness of their work. Conducting *ad hoc* investigations into the organization of clinical treatment is perhaps a task lacking the immediate priority of some of the other analyses which are expected of trust management. Of course it should also be recognized that investigations into doctors' working practices are a sensitive issue, encroaching on the profession's hallowed ground. For this reason the existence of a supportive clinical director is likely to be a crucial factor in allowing in-house 'Audit Commission style' studies to be carried out.

Professional owned and operated

The cautious manner in which medical audit was introduced after the 1990 Act was discussed in relation to primary care in Chapter 3. According to Pollitt (1993), the medical profession in the UK have been highly successful in preserving control over the medical audit process. This, however, remains a tool that medical or non-medical managers can admire from a distance but not acquire. Long-running profession-led audit programmes are in existence, most notably the National Confidential Enquiry into Perioperative Deaths which investigates the general quality of clinical work on a surgeon-by-surgeon basis. Drawing on the experience of these earlier national audits, the medical profession both at a national and local level have successfully 're-taken' medical audit after its apparent appropriation by the management process in Working for Patients (Campling *et al.* 1993). Pollitt's research (1993: 27) reveals that a 'medical model' has overlaid on the concept of medical audit. The profession have established the following principles:

- Only doctors shall conduct audit.
- Its main purpose shall be the education of doctors (i.e. it should be developmental and 'soft', not judgemental or regulative).
- Participation should be voluntary.
- 'Standards should be set locally by participating physicians' (ibid. p. 3).
- 'Open discussion cannot take place unless its confidentiality to the group is absolute'. The identity of the doctor whose work is being audited and the patients whose cases are being examined, must remain anonymous.
- The problem of doctors who regularly fall short of the standards agreed by the audit group 'is a medical, not a management problem'.

Comparison with the USA

The degree of the profession's secrecy and lack of acceptance of the need for audit to be used in the management of health service provision is only fully understood, according to Pollitt, when comparisons are made with the use of audit in the US health care system. Peer review as it is known in the USA is far more advanced in its development as a management technology than in the UK. In part, at least, this can be explained by the way in which remuneration terms and quality controls have become intertwined. It should be remembered that in the 'private' US health care system a considerable element of a doctor's income will be derived from the government funded Medicaid and Medicare programmes. Since the establishment of the Physician Payment Review Commission in 1985 to tackle the problem of doctors increasing their fees, an ever more sophisticated set of controls has been set in place (Oliver 1993: 124–6). In 1989, Congress ruled that the Medicare programme would discontinue its system of paying 'customary, prevailing, and reasonable' physician charges. In its place came a new fee schedule established on the basis of a new resource-based relative value scale. Importantly, this new scale rewarded on the basis of a standardized allowance for physician 'time and effort' associated with particular interventions. Most procedures are now covered by the relative value schedule for payment. This has the effect of making it unprofitable for a physician to carry out more procedures than are allowable.

Additionally, doctors are accustomed to being paid by insurers who traditionally imposed a regulatory regime through the bureaucracy involved in claiming fees for service. In the last ten years a high proportion of doctors have moved away from fee for service engagement in favour of a contractual relationship with 'managed care organizations'. A contractual relationship with a managed care organization will imply considerable monitoring of clinical practice. Also in 1989, the government established a new agency responsible for 'conducting, sponsoring and disseminating research on the costs and outcomes of medical procedures'. Indicating the importance of this initiative, the Agency for Health Care Policy and Research was given an initial budget of $62 million when it became operational (Oliver 1993: 156).

Increasingly accustomed to resource-based controls over their practice, US doctors are also subject to external peer review as participants in the Medicare programme. Since 1981 the scope of peer review has broadened and the newly created Peer Review Organizations (PRO) now examined issues of medical quality as well as identifying those unnecessary physician expenditures which their forerunners had concentrated on. PROs use a panel of physicians to investigate suspected cases of substandard care. Physicians deemed to have delivered substandard care are asked to provide an explanation and then may face a 'sentence' of re-education if they wish to continue practising. Pollitt notes the openness of the PRO-based system. Data is provided in a form that allows for comparisons to be made between providers.

Hospitals in the USA are under pressure to ensure that self-employed doctors given 'privileges' – a contract to use the hospitals facilities – work efficiently. The hospital is reimbursed for its part through the Prospective Payment System (PPS) according to the Diagnostic Related Groups system, which clusters medical interventions under together (DRGs). Around five hundred DRGs are in existence, each placing a limit on the type and volume of hospital resource use associated with a particular type of medical intervention (Davis and Rhodes 1988: 121–2). While the DRG system is open to abuse it nevertheless has introduced an element of external control over medical practice unknown in the UK. For the time being, British doctors have successfully prevented medical audit becoming the Trojan horse which allows externally driven performance analysis to influence their work.

Protocols

In the absence in the UK of equivalents of the resource-based relative value scale with its purpose of standardizing behaviour through a system of financial rewards based on a measurement of the 'time and effort' associated with particular medical treatments, or the DRG based constraints on treatment patterns, an interest has developed among doctors in clinical guidelines or clinical protocols. Protocols are being produced as a result of both national and local initiatives in developments that reflect the profession's growing interest in evidence-based health care. Clinical protocols are systematically developed statements whose purpose is to assist practitioner, and ultimately patient decisions about appropriate health care for specific medical conditions and circumstances (Grimshaw and Russell 1993).

Sheldon (1994: 34–5) sees the effectiveness of clinical protocols as being dependent on:

1 Validity – correct interpretation of evidence;
2 Cost-effectiveness – improving health;
3 Reproducibility – other groups can adapt;
4 Reliability – other health professionals apply similarly;
5 Representative development – key disciplines have contributed;
6 Clinical applicability – target population properly defined;
7 Clinical flexibility – allows for exceptions and patient preferences;
8 Clarity – precision in terminology;
9 Meticulous documentation – methods recorded and recommendations explained;
10 A built-in schedule for review.

The anticipated benefits of adopting clinical protocols are said to be an increase in appropriate practice resulting in reduced morbidity and mortality, improved efficiency through the control of excessive clinical action, and cost containment by targeting finite resources on effective interventions (Cluzeau 1994: 121–2). The use of clinical protocols also helps groups of health professionals share the care of patients, in establishing precisely each person's contribution. In situations where patients become litigious an ability to demonstrate that a protocol has been followed is clearly advantageous. In the context of the internal market it is possible that the trade between purchasers and providers could take place on the basis of protocols. Management of doctors and other health professionals through protocols is an established reality in some areas, asthma care being a noticeable example; but the care of the majority of patients and illnesses remains fragmented (Heymann 1994).

Best practice

In some centres doctors have formally agreed what constitutes best practice in terms of outcome criteria and indicators and systematically established 'bench marks' against which performance is to be assessed. The criteria used, according to Øvretveit should be outcome-orientated and include a measurement of health gain (Øvretveit 1992). Bench-marking is similar in methodology to the league tables produced by the Department of Health/Scottish Home and Health Department but is profession owned and managed. The focus is on individual clinician's performance rather than the trust or the specialty. The level of detail regarding clinical outcomes can be expected to greatly exceed that which is used in league tables and drawn on scientific evidence relating to best practice. It is up to individuals to compare their own or their team's performance against agreed best practice. It is feasible to envisage a voluntary pact arising between like-minded clinicians where they will collectively use bench-marking as a means of managing their performance. At present bench-marking is in a research and experimentation mode as opposed to a management mode and is carried forward by enthusiasts in the medical profession (Bulivant and Naylor 1992: 24–5).

Accreditation

Control over the process by which doctors are licensed to practice, although an obvious technology of performance control, has not been seen in management terms. Nevertheless, the question of accrediting doctors on a more systematic basis has become more prominent in the last few years. At least in part this is to be explained by the changing relationship between the doctors and their patients. The public are becoming more assertive both individually and collectively through pressure group activity. It is widely believed that the age of deference is over and the professions' governing bodies are under pressure to respond to a more assertive patient voice (Stacey 1992: 199).

GPs in particular, working outside the 'learning environment' provided by hospitals, are thought to be exposed to a problem of maintaining competence levels throughout their careers (Stanley and Al-Sheri 1993: 524–9). Doubts are frequently expressed over existing arrangements for accreditation – are they adequate to the task of managing competence levels in an age where patients have begun to see themselves as consumers?

The General Medical Council established the following competence criteria for general practitioners:

1 The ability to solve clinical and other problems in medical practice.
2 Possession of adequate knowledge and understanding of the general structure and function of the human body and workings of the mind in health and disease, of their interaction and of the interaction between man and his physical and social environment.
3 Possession of consultation skills.
4 Acquisition of a high standard of knowledge and skills in the doctor's specialty.
5 Willingness and ability to deal with common medical emergencies and with other illness in an emergency.
6 The ability to contribute appropriately to the prevention of illness and the promotion of health.
7 The ability to recognise and analyse ethical problems, so as to enable patients, their families, society and the doctor to have proper regard to such problems in reaching solutions.
8 The maintenance of attitudes and conduct appropriate to a high level of professional practice.
9 Mastery of skills required to work within a team and, where appropriate, assume the responsibilities of team leader.
10 Acquisition of experience in administration and planning.
11 Recognition of the opportunities and acceptance of the duty to contribute to the advancement of medical knowledge and skill.
12 Recognition of the obligation to teach others. (Southgate 1994: 88)

The profession's guardianship of standards has been concerned to guarantee minimum standards of performance. However, in the words of one commentator 'the genie of consumerism is out of the bottle'. Rather than simply maintain minimum standards, Stanley and Al-Sheri (1993) believe that the upwardly moving 'normative' expectations formed by patients, politicians and the media, need to be dealt with. In the case of GPs, professional competence was traditionally the responsibility of individuals rather than their Royal Colleges or other professional bodies. Continual re-accreditation throughout a GP's career may provide a means of shifting responsibility onto the profession. While post-graduate education for GPs has developed rapidly in many areas of the UK there is a lack of a real performance management dimension in the profession's approach to competence. Re-framing accreditation and post-graduate education in a management guise may prove to be a means by which the medical profession collectively demonstrates its competence.

It has been also been claimed that an impending crisis is looming through the readiness of doctors to try out new techniques without proper training. Surgeons were recently accused of dabbling in specialist operations without proper training. Key-hole surgery is said to be a particularly dangerous area, with surgeons too often learning on a 'see-one, do-one, teach-one' basis (Jones 1994). The medical profession may decide themselves to adopt a more proactive approach to accreditation. Alternatively, it may be forced on them by a future government. The system based on the General Medical Council and Local Medical Committees is not perhaps up to the demands that the public are beginning to make. Locally and nationally the profession's ability to 'self-regulate' is being questioned.

Additionally, there is now a direct financial incentive for trusts to regulate the safety aspects of care provided by doctors. In 1990 the NHS Management Executive adopted a similar approach to that being examined in the US by establishing NHS indemnity for all clinical staff. Consultants and junior staff are now free from financial worries regarding claims of negligence (Miller and Harrison 1993). The cost of claims now falls on trusts. Consultant relief is tempered by awareness that since trusts now bear the cost of poor quality care, managers are more interested in monitoring the quality of care delivered. There is now a keener interest in risk management and quality assurance by those outside the profession. This is a threat to clinical autonomy, which may possibly force a management dimension into the profession's regulatory systems.

In *The Incompetent Doctor*, Rosenthal (1995: 144–6) argues for the adoption of a comprehensive overall peer evaluation system that begins with the medical school admissions process and continues until retirement. She suggests such a system should include:

1 A more sophisticated medical school selection process that identifies the 'difficult' personality and the problem prone.
2 A commitment on the part of the medical schools to 'counsel' students with emerging problems into the most appropriate specialties or out of the field of clinical medicine.

3 Teaching and socializing a commitment to ongoing medical audit and peer review and self-scrutiny as a lifelong commitment of each individual doctor. Teaching stress management techniques.

4 More rigorous and systematic supervision of junior doctors to include a reduction of working hours to more realistic levels.

5 The institution of meaningful peer review mechanisms in every healthcare delivery unit, mechanisms that are more rigorous than the best that exist today; mechanisms that are a routine part of daily practice.

6 Support for regional centres of aggregated peer review data and clinical outcomes research to which every clinician gives data and from which every clinician receives data. Such centres would work to narrow the differences of opinion about diagnosis and treatment that exist between equal experts.

7 Support for the informal coping mechanisms as listed above; clearer delineation of responsibilities between the local medical committee and the FHSA and in the hospitals; more coordination of information and well-defined problem management techniques and time frames.

8 Professional training about the management of problem doctors for the Four Wise Men and for medical managers.

9 Incentives for earlier detection and help for impaired doctors.

10 Development of contracts that take potential problems into account by enumerating problems that are known to emerge, what informal mechanisms will be used, the help that will be offered to doctors with problems, and the formal mechanisms for suspending or ending contracts that exist.

11 A series of incentives for risk management programmes tied to Crown Indemnity or liability insurance, whether that insurance is paid by the individual, the hospital or a health-care management authority.

12 A regular cycle of re-licensing in seven-year cycles as required by a number of the American specialty colleges. This should include testing of not only current knowledge but where appropriate, skills as well. Developments in virtual reality applications to medical education should make this possible.

Even more radically, Maynard (1993b) has argued for doctors to be accredited both 'clinically and economically'. Alien as this may seem to doctors practising in the NHS it is an accepted part of the clinician's contract in some other health care systems most notably in the USA (see Chapter 7).

Quality management – the magic bullet?

Managers in the NHS as in all other organizations can be seduced by the attractions of quick-fix management systems. In the NHS during the 1990s a fair degree of interest has been expressed in relation to quality management. Quality management began life as a philosophy constructed around the ideas of the American management theorist Deming. Deming's ideas were particularly influential in Japan during the period of its post-war re-industrialization. Near the end of his life Deming summed up his philosophy of management in fourteen points:

1 Create constancy of purpose toward improvement of product or service, with the aim to become competitive and to stay in business, and to provide jobs.
2 Adopt the new philosophy. We are in a new economic age. Western management must awaken to the challenge, must learn their responsibilities, and take on leadership for change.
3 Cease dependence on inspection to achieve quality. Eliminate the need for inspection on a mass basis by building quality into the product in the first place.
4 End the practice of awarding business on the basis of price tag. Instead, minimise total cost.
5 Move toward a single supplier for any one item, on a long-term relationship of loyalty and trust.
6 Improve constantly and forever the system of production and service, to improve quality and productivity, and thus constantly decrease costs.
7 Institute training on the job.
8 Institute leadership. The aim of supervision should be to help people and machines and gadgets to do a better job. Supervision of management is in need of overhaul, as well as supervision of production workers.
9 Drive out fear, so that everyone may work effectively for the company.
10 Eliminate slogans, exhortations, and targets for the work force asking for zero defects and new levels of productivity. Such exhortations only create adversarial relationships, as the bulk of the causes of low quality and low productivity belong to the system and thus lie beyond the power of the work force.
11 (a) Eliminate work standards (quotas) on the factory floor. Substitute leadership.
   (b) Eliminate Management by Objective. Eliminate management by numbers, numerical goals. Substitute leadership.
12 (a) Remove barriers that rob the hourly worker of his right to pride of workmanship. The responsibility of supervisors must be changed from sheer numbers to quality.
   (b) Remove barriers that rob people in management and engineering of their right to pride of workmanship. This means, inter alia, abolishment of the annual or merit rating and of management by objective.
13 Institute a vigorous program of education and self-improvement.
14 Put everybody in the company to work to accomplish the transformation. The transformation is everybody's job.

(Deming 1988: 18–96)

Deming's ideas were clearly very radical when compared with standard thinking on management practices. His principles could have been dismissed as idealism were it not for the growing consensus that the Japanese economic miracle was founded on ideas broadly similar to those described by Deming. To import the principles into an organization like the NHS would involve a complete culture revolution. The principles he stressed have become adapted by 'followers' who in the 1980s formed the Total Quality Management (TQM) school. In the 1990s university business schools, management consultancies began teaching or selling a set of TQM derived concepts, tools and applications to the UK manufacturing industry and latterly to the service sector.

Summarizing the various definitions of TQM, Morgan and Murgatroyd (1994: 4–9) pick out the management of the customer–supplier chain of relationships as being at the heart of TQM. Customers can be people buying the finished product or members of the manufacturing team. Attention to satisfying the expectations of 'customers' whether end-product users or colleagues internal to the organization is what TQM strives to achieve. TQM is firmed up by reliance on data gathering and statistical methods to accurately measure customer satisfaction with product quality. In TQM processes, products and services are continually managed to meet changing patterns of customer needs and expectations.

Morgan and Murgatroyd (1994: 76) claim TQM works horizontally across professional disciplines and so 'inverts the management pyramid'. 'There are likely to be many, and possibly complex, customer–supplier chains'. They cite the example of delivering drugs to a patient, where a doctor, a nurse, a ward clerk, a porter and a pharmacist are all involved. They reject the view that the individual characteristics of patient care involve complex, one-off judgements on the part of doctors and other professionals, thus making the process of interaction hard to treat in a systematic fashion.

Doctors are used to working in teams, albeit in strictly hierarchical teams which are dominated by their discipline. TQM is a concept that has had an initial resonance in the administrative and nursing arms of the NHS. Whether it can be demonstrated to have made an impact is not clear. While implementation difficulties in experimental TQM sites were reported by Kogan and colleagues (1992) there is still a fair degree of confidence in those aspects of TQM which borrows on the statistical methods used in operations research. Øvretveit (1990: 132–3), for example, argues that a patient's journey through the health care system should be studied and worked up into a flow diagram depicting the stages which a patient passes through in time. This draws on the traditions of operations research.

TQM, according to Merry, would involve replacing retrospective reviews of individual patient charts with the analysis of statistical data, replacing the focus on individuals to 'epidemiological' perspectives. Instead of 'what went wrong with this individual case?' they ask 'what might be the common denominator of this high infection rate?' – location, organism, anatomical site of infection or the physician (Morgan and Murgatroyd 1994: 76–7). Kleefield *et al.* (1991: 138–43) also believe that quality in a hospital can be raised through process improvements in the hospital just as it can in any other industry.

It is also claimed that doctors have been amazed that customer audits reveal a different view of the quality of services they have provided and then prick up their ears as new converts to TQM (Morgan and Murgatroyd 1994: 73–4). Clearly, TQM must be grounded in a much deeper understanding of patients' needs and expectations. The experience in NHS demonstration sites seems to indicate that nurses, rather doctors, will be trained in customer audit. While the TQM devotees recognize the extent of the culture shock for doctors of the ideas they promote no real explanation is given as to why the profession will dance to the quality tune. Little interest in TQM has been forthcoming from the medical profession itself. There is little to suggest audit is being introduced into the formal training process undergone by doctors.

Customer audit, which must be central to any TQM process, is in its infancy. If placed in the hands of nurses or practice managers rather than doctors the inevitable prospect arises that customer audit becomes a bureaucratic business of getting the forms in on time rather than a process that becomes integral to the process of treating patients. If TQM is to work in any form it must be a system which has the full participation of doctors who are the key players in the process of patient care.

More positively, it should be recognized that customer audit is developing in the NHS, albeit from a very low base. For example, very few GPs have any experience of systematically recording their patients satisfaction with treatment in the hands of hospital colleagues and few hospitals are organized in a way that will systematically record and act upon records of customer satisfaction with treatment. However, quite large numbers of NHS trusts and primary care medical practices have successfully designed systems for monitoring consumer satisfaction in bidding to be awarded the Charter Mark. This is a government scheme which recognizes high quality standards in all types of organization (Horton and Farnham 1993: 32–9).

In the highly competitive US health care system health maintenance organizations (HMOs) compete with one another to win and retain patients. They have created fairly sophisticated means of monitoring patient satisfaction. For example, one small HMO, carries out patient surveys on a site or area basis four times every year. It sends 3500 questionnaires out and gets back around 800 each time. It also uses the telephone as a research tool analysing the type of queries or complaints that come in. Importantly, there is a very direct link between customer research and the management of doctors. If, for example, a patient calls up and says the doctor did not listen to her, the HMO would probably change the patient's next appointment to another doctor. The original doctor would be told that the patient had complained within two weeks, and be presented with a written report on the complaint. In this example, the HMO has a target patient retention figure. In its case it hopes that 90 per cent of patients will stay with it (interview with HMO customer care manager, April 1993).

The internal market has as yet failed to create the type of competitive environment where NHS managers must be driven to respond to consumer needs and expectations. One possible stimulus to action is the shock that may be revealed by investigations into NHS 'quality costs'. Quality costs in health care typically divide into four categories:

1 prevention costs, such as training in quality methods;
2 appraisal costs, such as those involved in obtaining patient feedback;
3 internal failure costs, such as communication breakdowns;
4 external failure costs, such as the cost of dealing with patient complaints. (Vonderemsbe and White 1991)

It is feasible to see quality cost investigations as a means of focusing management attention on clinical processes. However, the supporters of TQM argue that the system cannot be introduced on a piece-meal basis – it is all or nothing. Pollitt (1996) sees TQM as having worked in industry where firms have been in fairly desperate straits, with competitors ready to pounce. TQM is a high-risk strategy for desperate circumstances. The TQM enthusiasts fail to acknowledge that their philosophy, or at the very least its operational technologies must be endorsed by the professional bodies and built into the training of doctors. The situation in the NHS would appear to be some way off from the circumstances of desperation that a major TQM-based culture change would require.

Consumer driven management

Taken in a wider social context than that understood in TQM terms, consumer pressure may prove to be the environmental factor that pressurizes doctors into new types of performance management. This could take the form of 'defensive medicine' as allegedly practised by litigation fearing doctors in the USA. More positively, it is hoped by the consumer rights advocates that the NHS can be made to see the benefits of developing its awareness of how the public see it performing (Ranade 1994). The Citizen's Charter was launched by the Prime Minister John Major, with a view to introducing a degree of consumer rights not previously recognized in the public services in the UK. The NHS produced its own charter in 1991. The nine charter standards contained within the Patient's Charter, which the NHS in Scotland aimed to meet, were:

1 Respect for privacy, dignity and religious and cultural beliefs.
2 Arrangements to ensure everyone, including those with special needs, can use the services.

3 Relatives and friends to be kept informed about treatment, subject to patient's wishes.
4 Emergency ambulance should arrive within fourteen minutes in an urban area or nineteen minutes in a rural one.
5 Need for treatment assessed immediately in accident and emergency departments.
6 Specific appointment times in outpatient clinics and maximum waiting time of thirty minutes.
7 Where cancellation of operations happens twice in succession, the patient must be admitted within one month of the date of the second cancellation.
8 A named qualified nurse, midwife or health visitor responsible for each patient.
9 Planned discharge arrangements, which include provision for social care or rehabilitation needs of the patient.

(National Health Service in Scotland 1991)

Hogg and Cowl (1994) believed that the process by which standards were developed was more important to patients than the list of standards or rights. In their view charters should be seen as a part in quality raising projects involving GPs and hospitals working with patients and local people. Clinical audit and patients' surveys should be integrated into the process. It is argued that while the intention of the Charter was to enhance the patients' rights, in reality it is more likely to be useful to managers looking for standards to help negotiations and the contracting process. The 'activist' consumer rights tendency would like to see patients being involved in establishing the standards on which Charter rights are based (British Journal of Nursing 1994). It can also be argued that the Charter must include some significant standards on clinical outcomes. Pointing out again the problem of attention to waiting times, MacAlister (1994) suggests recovery rates following specific treatments, post-operative infection rates, nursing standards and a measure of the quality of hospitals is required.

To date it is unclear whether the publication of Charter standards has stimulated greater consumer awareness and willingness to complain. Critics question the ability of individual patients to press home complaints in a manner that causes doctors or hospitals to make changes. For others, the problem lies in the mechanics of making a complaint and subsequent responses by the NHS. Changes have been made in this area. In the office of Health Commissioner exists a means of attending to complaints without resort to the courts (Acheson 1991). It is a free independent service led by a commissioner with a staff of investigating officers drawn on secondment from the NHS and Civil Service. The Commissioner is responsible to Parliament who can decide what he can and cannot investigate and in Acheson's words, 'invest him with powers similar to that of a High Court in terms of enabling him to see documents'. In practice, the most common

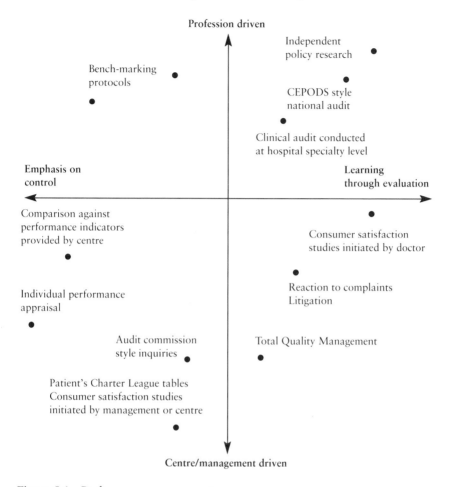

Figure 5.1 Performance management map

cause of complaint is said to be poor communications between professionals and patients. The Commissioner conducts investigations which are usually hospital based. As a service it is limited in influence as a channel for consumer pressure by the clause in its constitution which prevents the Commissioner examining cases believed to have arisen solely as a result of clinical judgement. In 1996, the NHS adopted the recommendations of the Wilson Report on complaints (General Practitioner 1994). The aims of the new system were to make it easier for people to complain by standardizing the system across the NHS. Greater responsibility was given to 'frontline' staff for dealing sensitively and quickly with complaints. Introducing the new complaints system in Scotland the Health Minister Lord James emphasized the need for managers to look on complaints as a valuable source of information (Press and Journal 1996).

Summary

This chapter has provided an introduction to the technologies of performance management as they currently relate to doctors in the NHS. We can
speculate as to the extent to which doctors will be increasingly the subject
of externally initiated controls or whether the profession will successfully
head off pressure by devising its own methods. As a means of simplifying
the performance management terrain, the range of technologies for managing doctors' performance are set out in Figure 5.1, which places the
systems or initiatives discussed above on a map according to four criteria:

- profession owned and managed
- centre/management driven – non-profession owned and managed
- research orientated
- control orientated.

The main purpose of this diagram is to illustrate the emptiness of the
top left quadrant described as profession driven–control orientated. The
bulk of performance management initiatives have an emphasis on control
but are centre or non-medical management driven. This negates their
current influence as tools for influencing the performance of doctors. The
extent to which the medical profession endorses bench-marking and clinical
protocols is likely to be important in the medium term. In the longer run,
consumerism may prove to be of significance.

6 Fit for purpose? Organization and medical management

The organization of the NHS is perhaps best understood as a creation made out of spare parts and make-do's – a political compromise between competing interests – rather than a purpose-built vehicle for delivering publicly funded health care. Previous chapters have charted the uneasy history of administrative centralization, professional dominance over operations culminating with the experiment with the internal market. Chapter 3 argued that the market certainly is not yet king and a traditional reliance on limited scope centralization is still evident in the actions of politicians and senior NHS managers. In addition, the creation of clinical directorates in NHS trusts as a means of managing doctors has been accommodated to some extent by the existing professional organization at specialty level, while the impact of performance management technologies is still uncertain. With little resolved in organizational terms doctors, still the dominant force in the NHS, have a number of alternative futures to contemplate. The viability of different organizational types is dependent on a complex range of factors in which the professional interests and instincts of doctors is ultimately likely to be the most important. This book is not directly concerned with health policy. In examining alternative organizational bases for delivering health care, the purpose here is rather to establish 'ideal types' with which existing and emergent organizational patterns can be compared.

Several organizational 'ideal types' are considered below. As a basic template Henry Mintzberg's by now standard classifications of different organizational designs have been used along with the work of writers dealing with various aspects of network organizations. At one end of the spectrum there is the familiar machine organization with its roots in production line management and at the opposite end lies the loose type of organization based on a dynamic network of informally interdependent players. Somewhere in between lies the rather imprecise location of real-life organizations, including the NHS. The purpose of establishing ideal types is to help focus on *aspects* of actual organizational life which may be significant as a pointer to how the NHS and medical management can or will develop. Before considering different organizational forms some key properties of medical organization should be established.

It can be argued that scientific management principles were never viable in a field of activity dominated by highly skilled professionals (Harrison *et al.* 1992: 14–17). Yet this is to miss a crucial feature of professional work, which is dominated by routine and repetition (Fogel 1989). Mintzberg's summary of different types of control found in organizations is useful in this respect (Mintzberg 1989: 95–106). He argues that organizations are not linear – a mistake made by many analysts. Instead we should be looking not at particular attributes so much as how attributes configure into 'gestalts'.

Adapting to the context of medical management in the NHS, six basic types of control may be said to be used:

1 *Mutual adjustment.* In the context of NHS medical management this describes collegiate relations which define detailed clinical responsibilities and informal communications including routine peer review. The emergence of a clinical management team is reliant on this style of control. This system requires participants to respect one another's professional judgements.

2 *Direct supervision.* One person issues the orders. Examples are to be found in the traditional clinical 'firm', headed by a consultant where medical and nursing roles are ascribed in hierarchical terms. This may be in decline as training grade doctors cease to be seen as responsible to particular consultants.

3 *Standardization of work processes.* This is heavily relied upon in the consultation process and in, for example, accident and emergency departments where a clear sequence will be established wherein a patient presenting themselves for treatment will initially be assessed by a nurse and subsequently passed through a chain of increasing clinical seniority. It is also relied upon in surgical and medical interventions. The potential need to justify actions in the event of a complaint ensures the importance of this type of control form in all health care systems. It is a means of reconciling clinical activity with the legal requirements demanded of the medical profession.

4 *Standardization of outputs.* It is often hard to calibrate health care outputs although proxies are referred to, such as days patients spend in post-operation recovery occupying beds. This is difficult to use in many areas of health care although individual clinicians or clinical teams, as opposed to departments, may have notional output standards which they refer to.

5 *Standardization of skills and knowledge.* Work is co-ordinated by virtue of related training. This is possibly the key means of controlling clinical activity. For example, an anaesthetist responds almost automatically to the surgeon's actions in an operating room. Continuing education is needed to maintain the effectiveness of this form of control.
6 *Standardization of norms.* Everyone functions according to the same beliefs. The 'soft' cultural dimension is developed in medical school/ hospital training. The extent of its use in the NHS is likely to vary from specialist area to specialist area. At a basic level it is used to control the basis of the doctor–patient relationship.

The important point is that medical work is controlled by standardization. It is not dominated by genuinely autonomous individual decisions. Decision-making parameters are in place in the form of the controls described above. The importance of clinical autonomy in the analysis of power relations in the NHS has obscured this aspect of health service organization as it relates to doctors. In consequence of the organizational gestalt or bias that has emerged the NHS, both primary and secondary sectors have organizational structures which help them work to an accepted standard. These structures have developed largely in isolation from the actions of hospital or health board managers. In the NHS the traditional and key control mechanisms are almost exclusively profession designed and operated. However, the multi-dimensional forms of control used in existing management of clinical behaviour mean that a broad range of organizational designs should be considered as part of the crystal ball gazing exercise on future directions which the NHS could potentially take. In the review that follows we consider:

- the machine organization
- the professional organization
- the network organization (three variants)
- the innovative organization.

Machine management and doctors

Hospital organization and health service provision in its wider context is not an immediately obvious candidate for production-line style people management.

Mintzberg (1989: 131–8) defines the machine organization as being based on highly specialized routine operating tasks. Characteristically very formalized communications are used throughout the organization. Machine organizations must be based on large-size operating units. There is a reliance on a functional basis for grouping work tasks. Heavily centralized power relations predominate in the decision-making process – an aspect of organization emphasized by the complexity of hierarchical arrangements and the sharp distinction between managerial staff and line workforce. Production line machine organizations are not attractive places for well-educated professionals to operate, yet the rewards of designing an organization with the characteristics outlined above can be great and not confined to the industrial world of 'long chimneys and heavy boots'. Machine organization was quickly replicated in white-collar industries such as insurance services where low cost, routine and predictability of action were keys to success. Witness also the use of an adaptation of the machine-style organization in the operations of McDonalds – the world's most successful fast food chain. McDonalds competitive advantage comes from control over costs, standardization of product and reliability.

Certain types of clinical work can quite easily be measured according to cost, conformance to standards and reliability. By adopting machine organization as an operating principle, the NHS would be redesigned, eliminating the autonomy granted to units under the internal market and redefining clinical autonomy. This would not be a return to a pre-Working for Patients state. Machine organization could only work were doctors prepared to take up the key posts in the management hierarchy and also the supervisory roles in the line workforce.

A medical managerial elite at the apex of the organization would be responsible for developing a clinical flow line for treating patients – analogous to a production line. However, technologically advanced machinery is unlikely to provide the basis for controlling performance in the major areas of clinical work. With a few exceptions the introduction of machinery has never realized principles of automation in health care. Certainly the type of de-skilling fulfilled in the automotive industry in the first half of this century is unlikely to be achieved. For example, Henry Ford was, by 1922, in a position to assess jobs on his production line according to how many limbs the worker needed to carry out the physical tasks involved. There were 7882 separate tasks in the manufacture of Ford's cars. Out of these 670 could be performed by legless men, 2637 by one-legged men, 2 by arm-less, 715 by one-armed men and 10 by blind men. Out of the total of 7882 jobs, 4034 did not require full physical capacity (Littler in Knights *et al.* 1985: 15).

The flow line could instead be clinical protocol and performance indicator based. Doctors need skills but wherever possible they should work according to a set of highly detailed rules. De-skilling is perhaps a misnomer for doctors who would be required to learn new skills in working to protocol-based medicine. Of course it has never been an objective in the British or American health care systems to explicitly de-skill jobs through automation or other means, yet undoubtedly a certain potential exists in at least some areas of medicine. The type of clinical work that is adaptable to machine organization is currently seen as being confined to the type of interventions where relatively consistent sets of problems are encountered – the removal of cataracts for instance.

To extend machine organization into less obvious areas would require the development of a large centralized 'technostructure' capable of standardizing medical procedures to an extent not seen in the NHS to date.

Mintzberg provides a standard technostructure cast list consisting of analysts, schedulers, quality control engineers, planners, budgeters, accountants, operations researchers whose contributions could at least potentially be replicated in the NHS. This technostructure would create the medical flow line, providing the list of tightly specified tasks to be undertaken, the line staff roles, line staff supervisory roles, the terms of supervision and the rules for supervisors and also the rules for resolving inevitable conflicts when cases do not quite fit the flow line. In health services, if this is the route that is to be taken, a new category of technostructure physician will be needed to help create meaningful rules that provide the basis for controlling medical care to a satisfactory degree of accuracy. At present few physicians would have the skills or experience to perform this vital task. The type of epidemiological and planning skills acquired by, for example, a public health physician are simply not specific enough for this role. Doctors who were themselves specialists would be required to work with operational research experts, and quality control engineers to work up the highly detailed rules that are required by the machine organization. The aim of the machine is to take the discretion away from the doctors who actually treat patients and limit their responsibility to that of keeping within very specific guidelines on how a particular case should be approached. Similarly, a large number of line managers would need to be employed to enforce the rules emanating from the technostructure. While some line managers could be recruited from perhaps the nursing profession or from general management backgrounds, it seems clear that supervision would require an input from another new category of managers – doctors who are appointed as supervisory managers to lead the middle line hierarchy. A third type of managerial role for doctors would emerge in the murky area of 'fixing'. Fixers are necessary to sort out disputes over rules, disputes between sub-units and supervisors, and to reconcile competing interests. Some might conclude that such a role already exists in the NHS.

Much energy will be consumed in the machine organization simply controlling its mechanisms. Innovative practice can only be introduced after the technostructure has worked through its analysis and specification processes. An unreformed medical profession would be unable to provide the manpower to first standardize medical work and then supervise operational processes. A massive skills deficit would exist and this would be compounded by a predictable lack of inclination to give up traditional medical career patterns to specialize in technostructure work or develop management skills for the supervisory hierarchy.

Specialization and calculability – the ability to quantify activities – are seen as key determinants in centralizing power in the hands of managers at the apex of organizations. In spite of obstacles inherent in the simplified scheme discussed above, it is possible to argue that the trend in modern medicine towards greater specialization with all specialties dividing into a complex arrangement of sub-specialties, each with their own procedures, produces an ever more amenable set of clinical activities for the standardizers to work on. The machine organization would therefore favour or be dependent on a particular philosophy of health care.

Professional organizations

Health services are depicted as classic professional organizations alongside other notable examples such as law and accountancy partnerships. This type of structure is designed to allow professionals the discretion to react as they see fit to particular contingencies that arise. It includes a built-in bias to support the one-to-one interactions that professionals tend to have with their clients. Professionals are employed on the basis of standard minimum training and can be expected to react to problems according to commonly understood principles that have been instilled in them. The structures found in professional organizations are a response to the relative complexity and non-standardized problems that are encountered. There will typically be less emphasis on vertical communications – instructions issued from above – and more reliance placed on horizontal communications between professional equals.

Professional organizational structures may co-exist alongside machine organization structures within single organizations such as a hospital, tasks being assigned to each structure according to the type of work involved. It can be easily argued that the delivery of health care takes place in one organization within another organization – a professional bureaucracy within an administrative bureaucracy. For example, job specialization is professionally designed. Medical, nursing and support staff relate to one another according to a type of bureaucracy imposed through job specialization. The professions formalize behaviour. This takes the form of operating instructions, job descriptions, rules and regulations governing conduct. Medicine is increasingly becoming bureaucratized through the use of clinical protocols. The medical profession have traditionally provided the meaningful means of liaising between the different clinical sub-units within hospitals. Bureaucracies rely on grouping roles together in hierarchical reporting arrangements. Professional organizations rely on a less hierarchical form of unit grouping. A grouping process nevertheless still forms the basis by which professionals placed together in sub-specialty units, interact. This grouping process also forms the pattern through which those units are integrated into higher clinical orderings on which hospital life depends.

Professional organizations are special types of bureaucracies that are both tightly bound by rules and at the same time decentralized. The work they engage in has been thought to be too complex to be handled by a technostructure, hence the need to empower professionals on the ground. The core activities carried out by the professionals themselves have typically been subject to an 'arm's length form of management'. Frequently, key operational procedures are 'internalizations' of practices defined by professional bodies rather than the actual employers of professionals. By employing professionals the employer is being at least partly released from the need to ensure its employees stay within the law. Compulsory membership of professional bodies ensures that practising professionals are subject to common rules. Professionals react to problems according to well-understood principles that are instilled in them in the training and accreditation process. This has proved to be an effective type of quality control mechanism.

A degree of behaviour normalization is evident in the professionals' organizational life. Procedures learnt as trainees become enforced as repetitive practice and reflex actions which are important means of building in safety and quality controls over professional services. Nevertheless, in spite of the robustness of the professional organization as a guarantor of quality and safety in an increasingly competitive business environment, professionals are quickly realizing that a management challenge confronts them. Both machine and professional organizations are designed for conditions of relative calm. The machine organization works on the basis of rules created by its technostructure while the professional organization is regulated by the common training backgrounds and values of its members. Neither is well suited to rapidly changing political or economic demands or for exploiting new technological possibilities. Professional organizations are not readily responsive to strategic management. The stress on professional training ensures that a degree of self-reliant individualism is evident. This is both a strength and a weakness. The need to devolve decision-making powers to self-reliant professionals takes power away from would-be commander-strategists. Changes in behaviour may take a generation to work through the organization, given the reliance on training as a means of ensuring control over procedures and standards. Yet such is the ambiguity present in interpretations of organizational design that theorists see the professional organization as a special type of 'flat bureaucracy', which is specially suited to changing course quickly. The flat organization is worthy of some consideration in relation to the management of doctors.

In an article that directly argues for business organizations to become more like hospitals, Drucker (1988) cites the historical precedent of the British Empire's Indian Civil Service which ran the subcontinent with a few hundred staff who enjoyed substantial delegated authority. A more contemporary example of the flat professional organization is provided by another management guru Tom Peters (1993: 31–43), in the form of the CNN news broadcasting organization. Peters describes CNN as an 'unglued' organization whose leaders had rejected hierarchical management in favour of a system that gave responsibility to the ground level professionals gathering news as it happened. CNN had dispensed with the journalists' reliance on deadlines to control news gathering efforts. CNN is on-line 24 hours a day. Symbolically CNN's founder Ted Turner felt no need to establish prestigious headquarters in America's seats of political and economic power, Washington and New York. Based in Atlanta Georgia, the CNN headquarters are small with nothing lavish about the building or offices to suggest this is the heart of a corporate empire. Peters enthused about the manner in which decisions were taken at CNN. Turner and his immediate deputies are around on the floor and not up in some plush office away from the action. Decisions of great magnitude get taken by three or four people, not by committees, because there are no committees. Decision making on the run is normal rather than a symptom of stress.

To make the system work, CNN got rid of the idea that big name 'star' reporters were needed to front the station. A new category of employee – the video journalist – was created. The old networks have a long list of people in their news crews and the reporter is the top of a professional sub-unit hierarchy. In CNN the video journalist is expected to be a competent handler of technical matters and will only have a cameraman and a sound recordist with him. Video journalists are multi-skilled and bereft of status-marking symbols to mark their position in the news gathering effort. Each video journalist is kept aware of the budgetary consequences of news gathering decisions they make. There is no distant accounts department. CNN is cost conscious but the key driver is self-control, not regulation.

If Peters' description is accurate then CNN and organizations like it are another variant on the professional organization theme having re-invented principles of self-reliance for modern business and technical challenges. For some observers, there is enough of the flat organization principle, the 'unglued organization' style, already evident in the NHS to make this a key guide to the future development of the medical management process.

Network organization

From the 1980s onwards large-scale business corporations increasingly perceived their scale of operation and administrative complexity as a disadvantage. Many business giants have seen their fortunes dip in markets where the running is being made by smaller, administratively lighter and more consumer-responsive competitors. Attempts to deal with this problem increasingly involved concepts such as 'outsourcing', 'hollowing-out', 'focusing on core business' and creating 'spin-offs' (Goffee and Scase 1995: 160). Handy (1989) recognized the 'startling discontinuity' in the language used to describe organizations. He notes that we no longer readily apply the engineering metaphors of old: structures, systems, inputs, control devices. Discussions about organizations now revolve round words like network, culture and influence. This is partly a recognition of the reality of contemporary business organization and part wishful thinking about what they should look like. There is an interesting argument that the NHS employs doctors whose experience of conducting operational relations with colleagues contains the antecedents of the network organizational life. This oddly enough may have little current congruence with the Working for Patient's devised internal market.

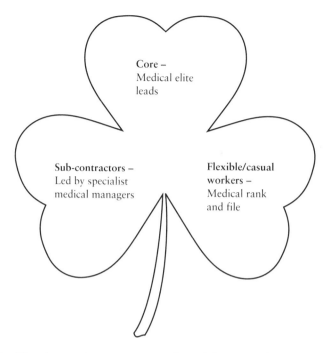

Figure 6.1 The shamrock organization (adapted from Handy 1989)

Stable networks

In a much quoted book, Handy (1989: 70–92) uses the idea of a three-'leafed' shamrock to describe the organization of the future (Figure 6.1). The first leaf represents the core workers, whose professional or technical status guarantees them security of employment and high financial reward. This group is crucial to the new style organization; without their expertise nothing can be achieved. The first leaf of the health service shamrock would be the organizational core based on a medical-managerial elite. The core would be constructed on a very short hierarchical ladder, perhaps no more than three rungs in length. Ideally, core staff in the shamrock organization relate to one another as equals, as partners in the enterprise, whether they are the de facto owners or not. Within the core, promotion is unusual – there being little in the way of a career ladder to climb. Reward is based on achievements and will take the form of profit sharing or bonuses rather than promotion. The basic role of the medical-managerial core would be to construct a health strategy, specify contractual targets and set charges for purchasers. Other than through managing terms of contract there would be no formal mechanism for controlling the sub-contractors who actually treat patients. Accreditation could be 'contracted out' on something similar to the current arrangement or become a core function.

However, the core workers are expensive and a feature of organizational life in the 1980s was the constant questioning of the value of contributions being made by middle management. The result was that corporate staff experienced redundancy and rejection from the organizational home just as blue-collar workers had done ten years earlier. (The timing of this re-structuring in industry in the UK, reflected a general backwardness in economic life and only seriously begun in the 1990s.) Turned out of the organizational home these middle-class professionals and technicians have moved into the second leaf of the shamrock – the realm of the sub-contractors. Corporations have always sub-contracted out some of the work involved in producing goods and services but by the 1990s leading edge corporations had demonstrated the effectiveness of the arrangement on a larger scale. A much quoted figure refers to the 20/80 split in Japan whereby 20 per cent of the workforce are in secure 'core' employment while 80 per cent work for sub-contractors. Clearly, this has enormous social significance in redefining the connection between class, qualifications and security of lifestyle.

The third leaf of the shamrock is formed by the 'flexible labour force', people dependent for their livelihood on the precarious rewards of part-time and temporary work secured from sub-contractors. Again this group has always existed in certain industries such as the building trade. It is now set to become a significant component in the structure of most if not all organizations. The third leaf already exists in the NHS, with a more or less flexible labour force having been created through the contracting out process that went on in the 1980s. At present it includes the people employed to clean hospitals, feed patients and maintain buildings. It is perfectly reasonable in economic terms for the nurses and junior medical staff to be hired on a flexible basis thus expanding this component of the NHS. Again this would not be a complete leap into the dark since to a limited extent this already happens in certain areas of the NHS, locums and agency nurses being hired on this basis. Sub-contracting answers some logical enough questions. Why not, for instance, hire nurses and doctors when they are needed to reflect the seasonal nature of acute health care needs?

Perhaps the whole health service could be coordinated on this basis. Existing NHS managers, however, probably do not have the professional skills required. This type of system does not support a large number of middle managers. Instead a new category of medical sub-contractor would need to be created in the second leaf of the shamrock. The sub-contractors would, if the experience with similar arrangements in the USA is replicated, come from the ranks of the hospital consultants. It is hard to dispute that doctors do not already have the basic knowledge to act in this capacity. In such a situation medical career choices would become much more complex than at present. High rewards could be gained in either leaf of the shamrock. The skills needed, however, would be very different.

Probably the medical 'firm' or 'clinical team' would be the basic sub-unit in the contracting leaf. The 'firm' being created on an *ad hoc* basis to fit the terms of the contract being undertaken. Experience with sub-contracting in other service industries such as architecture would suggest that the 'firm' would actually tend to be a fairly stable workgroup. The sub-contractors earn their profits through results – they are not rewarded on the basis of status or hours worked. The technology and accommodation required to practice medicine is expensive and there would be a strong economic incentive to pass the risk of investment onto the sub-contractors. Reacting to this problem, or rather this opportunity, a type of sub-contractor not involved in 'operational' medicine might enter the organization as a leaser of technology and facilities. Some doctors would become sub-contractors managing a firm and bidding for work, others would be in the flexible labour market picking up work that suited their needs and abilities, still others would move from being sub-contractors to casual members of a firm on an ongoing basis as it suited them.

An NHS based around a small operating core contracting out clinical operations may prove to be the eventual outcome of the internal market reforms. Certainly it is easy to portray the more successful aspects of the NHS of the 1990s as a type of internal network organization. The attempts to delineate more clearly between the trusts in their role as providers and the strategic contribution made by the newly created purchasing authorities, formed in England by the merger of Family Health Service Associations and District Health Authorities, may prove to be significant in the move towards a network form of organization (Ferlie and Pettigrew 1995: 376–84).

Politically, it may prove insurmountably difficult to move beyond the type of stable internal network that seemed to be envisaged in Working for Patients. The new purchasing authorities remain as organizations that still rely on large numbers of middle-junior managers to carry out their functions. The trusts also continue as organizations employing very large numbers of people in middle-junior management positions. Neither purchasing nor providing is managerially led by doctors. A criticism of the internal market from a 'network' perspective is that it is dominated by institution-to-institution relationships as opposed to clinician-to-clinician relationships. Another problem is posed by the harsh division in British medicine between primary and secondary care. The division may undermine the whole basis of an internal network. At worst the internal market will deliver none of the supposed benefits of a network – a core business focused concentration on health strategy with low management costs, flexibility and operational closeness to the customer – while incurring unnecessary transaction costs as ineffectual contracts are regulated by middle managers lacking knowledge of the clinical work being traded.

Dynamic networks

For a health service network to pay off in the sense of delivering better quality, better access and more innovation may require a more ruthless

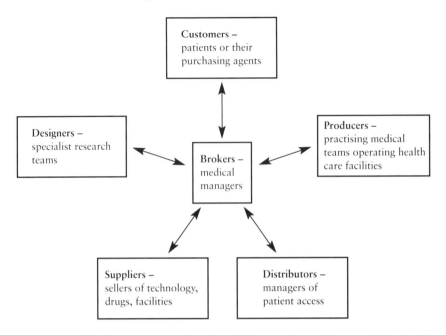

Figure 6.2   The dynamic network (adapted from Miles and Snow 1986: 62–72)

organizational revolution than that acceptable to government. According to Miles and Snow (1986: 62–72), successful networks are dynamic. They are led by active brokers at the centre of a moving web of relationships, held together on the basis of relationships that go beyond that found in contracts. The enriching device of 'full disclosure information systems' allow all parties to understand each others' interests and capabilities. In Figure 6.2, the Miles and Snow model is set out with health service identities attached to the players. In the dynamic network model the broker role and leadership of other parts of the network require specialized medical knowledge. Information pertinent to the work being carried out must not be used to gain advantage by either party to the contract. Old style business relationships based on a mix of commercial secrecy and trust borne of partnership longevity are not therefore the basis of dynamic networks.

Unless managed carefully such open-book relationships may actually be suppressed by the NHS internal market as purchasers seek to gain advantage in contractual relations. There is a threat in any trading relationship of opportunistic behaviour (Roberts 1993). Ensuring that the terms of the agreed contract are not undermined by either opportunist behaviour in the process of making the contract or in the delivery of the contract is necessary for networks to work. An example would be a provider in the network failing to deliver an 'expected' though not contractually stipulated level of service quality or, alternatively, a purchaser deceiving a provider into believing a lower level of demand was likely. In both cases commercial advantage can be gained by the opportunistic party through concealing information, but this is to the detriment of the success of the network.

More generally excellent quality of information and slick communications are essential for networks to deliver results. In economists' terms the network must be managed to avoid 'impactedness', that is ensuring that access on the part of a purchaser to service provision information is not dependent on the relationship with a particular individual, for example a doctor, or other professional, who has acquired a monopoly of information through length of service.

The backlash against 'downsizing'

Another danger exists in the Working for Patients experiment with a form of networking, in that far from encouraging innovative practice the institutional separation of purchasers from providers may stifle opportunity to develop new ideas in health care. At worst, cost-conscious market relationships could place a wedge between the primary care doctors and their specialist colleagues in the secondary sector. Within trusts increased pressure on patient-led resources could potentially damage relationships between specialists who need to co-operate in clinical processes.

This contradicts the association routinely made by the New Right advocates of Working for Patients between the creation of NHS trusts and GP fundholders and creativity. Certainly the size of bureaucratic units in the NHS has been reduced by the purchaser provider split. However, we may have been sold a small business myth about the inverse relationship between innovation and scale of organization. The Tom Peters (1993: 293) view for instance is typical of a very up-beat appreciation of the role of the networked organization in the end of mass production. The Japanese reliance on sub-contractors and the strength of the *mittelstand* medium-sized firm sector in the efficient German economy are cited as proof of the theory of networks. The big companies are taking a beating from the 'little guys' for the first time because networks have changed the definition of 'big'. The ability to react to secure niche markets is the terrain on which industrial battles are fought. This is a type of competition that demands scope of operation, the ability to create new products, rather than sheer size and economies of scale. Directly contradicting Peters is evidence on the innovation-stifling effects of 'down-sizing'. Dougherty and Bowman (1995) claim that managers are typically using downsizing simply to reduce costs and not to realize the potential of networks. They point out that 'a competitive cost structure only buys you a ticket to the game'. If the 'game' is all about innovation then downsizing is not the answer. In any case laid-off staff are often replaced by more expensive consultants bought in on contract terms to replace their contribution. Downsizing organizations hinders 'strategic linking activity' needed to carry organizational or product innovations through. They argue an entrepreneurial network has to exist to:

• sell the project to enough people, keep it alive and make it seem right for the company
• acquire resources for development
• get senior management commitment
• allow innovators to be able to work the system – a 'network' is not necessarily a system that allows for the pooling of knowledge on how to work the system
• allow innovators to work the system using personal credibility and influence, you need to understand how a product links with the firm's structure and strategy.

Considering the NHS and the management contribution required of doctors it becomes less and less easy to see the internal market as it stands as an organizational answer. The internal market is played at the wrong level – institutional as opposed to clinical – it is also led by non-medical managers.

Clan networks

Networks may yet form the basis of successful organizational redesign in the NHS. An aspect of organizational relations, which in the past has usually been overlooked, is related to the trust that exists between people who work together on a regular basis. Organizations where trust plays an important part have recently received some attention and have been studied with reference to the concept of the 'clan'. This is an entirely different basis on which to construct a network than that provided by market-based contracts. Doctors rely on trust relationships and 'clan' principles may be an important feature of health service organization which have been overlooked in the context of market-orientated rhetoric in the NHS.

In explaining the notion of clans in organizational life, Alvesson and Lindkvist (1993) make some points of relevance to the position of doctors in the NHS. Under certain circumstances both hierarchy or markets may be costly ways of regulating behaviour. While bureaucracies and hierarchies prohibit opportunistic behaviour, markets demand it. Opportunism is acceptable up to a point but may cause costly antagonisms to arise between the players in organizational life. Attempts should be made, it is argued, to find a third way of controlling behaviour that is both non-bureaucratic and non-market based. Where it is clear that neither bureaucracy nor the market function very well, the 'clan' provides the informal means of control which will emerge naturally or be nurtured as the basis for solving the organization's problems. There are two basic types of clan. The social integrative clan is a form of exchange relationships which we are familiar with in our non-organizational lives. It is a traditional group drawing on 'blood kinship, its members' sense of satisfaction, communion and belongingness'. Secondly, and of more relevance to the medical profession, there is the economic clan. The economic clan relies on high levels of 'goal congruence', members sharing the same corporate goals and indicators of personal success. On this basis help given to colleagues' efforts to achieve personal goals in the form of favours are made on a regular basis. While this may mean the 'favour giver' is under-rewarded in the short run, in the long run there is confidence in the clan to even out the effort-reward ratio. Part of the clan culture is the acceptance of uneven rewards being available at any one time, but faith in the system to even things out in the long run. The clan requires people to unite in a positive sense for long-term mutual gain.

The negative aspect of clan networks comes in the form of a degradation of market dynamics. In particular 'pair bonding' relationships may develop where the existing contract holder uses the close relationship with the purchaser to advantage. This may be indicated by situations where a personalized means of communication has developed between purchaser and provider. In this case it will be difficult for another provider to contest the bidding process. Roberts (1993) notes that the loss of the disciplinary edge of the market may lead to slack standards on contract delivery. In this case health gains will be lost. On the other hand, pair bonding may provide the stability that is needed for co-operative practices that result in health gains.

Innovative organizations

At the opposite end of the spectrum from the machine organization are those organic organizations whose structures are created to respond to the highly unpredictable technological advances and 'boundless' market opportunities that characterize their business environments. These types of organization are dedicated to innovation above all else. In direct contrast to the machine organization their structures are based on informal patterns of authority, where roles can quickly be redevised and power given to those individuals with the right skills and abilities for the task in hand. To try to play by set rules in highly turbulent business environments would be fatal to success. Mintzberg (1989: 196–220) has described the structural characteristics of the innovative organization as blurring the distinction between different posts. Project teams composed of essentially equal players are the basic organizing unit rather than hierarchies. In the innovative organization there is uncertainty and ambiguity, the structure resembles an umbrella that encourages individuals and sub-units to innovate within broadly defined 'value' parameters. This is an alien structure as far as most public service professionals are concerned, but once again it is possible – most likely in research contexts – to locate innovative style organizations operating as units within the NHS.

Organization for innovation is only suited to circumstances where taking risks is an acceptable part of management's strategy. The NHS may increasingly be in a position where goals and strategies have to be influenced by service innovation as opposed to the traditional perceived need to provide services of a uniform nature. Organizational structures may have to change accordingly shifting the emphasis away from reliance on rules and professional norms and encouraging innovation instead. There is a heavy reliance on individual initiative in these organizations. The originators are the teams or sub-units that are growing ideas. Managers are there to cultivate some ideas and kill off others, not to initiate. They could conceivably be drawn from non-medical backgrounds. A strategy only emerges through the process of picking winners. Where control was heavy and expensive in the machine organization, communication is heavy and expensive in the innovative organization, since managers require protected time for discussion that may often be 'fanciful' and unproductive, in order that a process of sharing ideas is stimulated. Innovative organizations are inefficient in strict economic terms since they rely on an idea rearing and culling process that is necessarily wasteful of resources.

Evaluating organizational types

The organizational types reviewed above are evaluated in Table 6.1 according to the following criteria:

- controlling costs
- outcomes orientation
- efficiency in consumption of management energy
- NHS compatibility
- involvement of doctors at the operational level
- dependency on elite medical leadership
- risk to government.

Controlling costs

If controlling costs is the primary requirement of an organization then the heavily regulated machine organization should be considered as a basic design model. Professional organizations with their reliance on routine and training-based repetitive behaviour are also likely to do reasonably well in relation to controlling costs. With resource consuming behaviour in the professional organization being, to a large extent, controlled at arm's length by an accreditation body rather than the local management, cost control is less precise than in the machine organization. A stable contract network as discussed above is an alternative to the machine organization. Use of casual employees lowers fixed costs in comparison with the machine organization. The dynamic network is, by definition, unpredictable but definitely not designed with cost control as a prime feature. Clan organization is again not focused on cost control – preserving trust in relations with

Table 6.1 Evaluating organizational types from a medical management perspective

	Machine organization	Professional organization	Stable contract network	Dynamic contract network	Clan network	Innovative organization
Control costs	High	Medium	High	Low	Medium	Low
Outcomes orientation	Low	Medium, but can be high	Medium	High	Medium, but can be high	High
Energy consumed in managing	High	Low at point of delivery – but training costs concealed	Low, provided parties to contract 'self-regulate'	Low although brokerage costs may be high	Low but hard to calculate	Low
NHS compatibility	High if controlled by profession	High – already proven	Medium – dependent on political climate	Low	Medium or low, hampered by administrative structure and primary secondary split	Low
Involvement of doctors at operational level	Low	Low	High if contractors, low if staff	High	High	High
Dependency on elite medical leadership	High	Medium	High	Low	Low	Low
Risk to government	Medium	Low	Medium	High	Low	High

colleagues may be more important than containing use of resources. Provided 'pair bonding' (see above) is not allowed to emerge, then the clan system of shared values can be seen as a basis for responsibility over the use of resources. Innovative organization types are not cost-conscious in a systematic sense. Cost control is exercised through the 'culling' process whereby projects deemed as failures are killed off.

Outcomes orientation

In relation to keeping outcomes in organizational focus, the machine organization's design means that it cannot be readily adapted to the pursuit of new target outcomes. The machine organization is dedicated to producing standardized outputs. Originally the technostructure will have designed outputs to meet intended outcome targets, which in the private sector are usually expressed in sales totals and profits. If standard specification outputs become less popular then outcomes are not achieved. A cumbersome process of redesign is needed to correct this failure. A bias is likely to exist for management to focus on producing outputs to order rather than achieving outcomes. By direct contrast innovative organizations and dynamic networks are readily adjustable to new outcome targets. They derive their purpose from the focus they can achieve on outcomes. Stable contract networks are a compromise in the sense that while sub-contractors can be rewarded on the basis of results, thus securing a high degree of outcome orientation, there is also the need to preserve an element of continuity which may mean less focused behaviour is tolerated in the short run. Professional organizations and clans have a considerable outcome orientation potential in the sense that training and shared values emphasize outcomes as opposed to outputs. Training may need to be managed in a more proactive manner if this potential is to be realized.

Efficiency in consumption of management energy

Machine organizations are high consumers of management energy. Technostructures and supervisory chains soak up resources. The professional organization is difficult to estimate in terms of its consumption of management energy. Although the professionals require minimum supervision at the point of service delivery there is the cost of training to be considered. The stable contract network is a low management energy consumer provided the players in the contracting process do not tend towards opportunistic behaviour which has to be policed. In one sense, the dynamic network is not really managed at all and is therefore very efficient. Brokerage costs incurred between parties to the network need to be taken into calculations but this may prove difficult. The innovative organization has no inclination to supervise its project teams, preferring instead to pick winners.

NHS compatibility

The 'classic' organizational types reviewed in this chapter lend themselves in varying degrees to the demands of managing health service provision. It has been argued that machine style organization is viable where the technostructure and much of the supervisory chain is staffed by the medical profession. Health service organizations have typically drawn on profession-provided organization to secure operational effectiveness. Stable contract networks and clan networks are means by which a greater degree of responsiveness can be built into organizational design. Dynamic networks and innovative organizations offer none of the trust relationships that doctors typically rely on.

Involvement of doctors at the operational level and dependency on elite medical leadership

Doctors have a degree of implied involvement in management that is dependent on the type of organization used. Machine organizations need the high involvement of a medical elite to operate their technostructure based command controls. Supervisory contributions are made by doctors in the flow line, but doctors who actually treat patients would not be required to take management decisions. Professional organizations require low involvement in management from doctors at the operational level, management contributions are made at the level of accreditation and training by a medical elite. By contrast, network organizations whether stable, clan-based or dynamic all rely heavily on the decision-making capabilities of doctors close to the patient to fuel their management processes. Lower dependency on medical elites is anticipated in these types of organization on the basis that much power over management decision making is ceded to the grass roots.

Risk to government

The NHS is ultimately the responsibility of elected politicians. Organizational types carry with them varying degrees of associated risk. Operating the NHS as a machine organization carries with it a medium risk. The safety of regulation and control over costs is counterbalanced by the high dependency on a medical elite succeeding in constructing an effective technostructure. The machine offers little capacity for manoeuvre once 'set up'. Professional organizations and clans are low risk politically since much of the perceived responsibility for actual service delivery can be shifted onto the medical profession. Both professional organizations and clans are also characteristically stable. The stable contract network as envisaged in Working for Patients is a medium risk, with the possibility of a low risk if blame can be shifted away from the elite decision makers in the core organization onto the sub-contractors delivering services. Innovative organizations and dynamic networks offer no stability and are high risks for government.

Conclusion

In the US health care system doctors are rapidly moving away from a traditional professional style of organization and becoming absorbed into managed care networks. The managed care organizations exploit many of the advantages of networks discussed above. The NHS is at present unable to create a network for the doctors to develop. The internal market, while superficially having the characteristics of a network, is not producing the advantages of this form of organization. If the internal market is a network, then it is a network of agencies and hospitals, rather than individuals or departments. As such it is too remote from the doctors who deliver services to reap the benefits of the network alliance. The NHS is still heavily reliant on traditional forms of organization rooted in professional and administrative tradition. The technologies of performance management examined in the previous chapter if properly developed can be made to drive other forms of organization. At worst this means an economy-orientated style of machine organization. Most radically a type of health care network as already in existence in the US could be fashioned in the UK.

7 Doctors and health service management – re-inventing the relationship?

Everywhere I go, the senior people tell me of progress, of better working methods and value for money, of objectives achieved, of changes delivered. Everywhere I go, I also glimpse another world, a world inhabited apparently by every-one else – a world of daily crisis and concern, of staff under pressure and services struggling to deliver. Both worlds are real in the minds of those who inhabit them. Both worlds are supported by objective evidence. Both views are held sincerely.

(Jarrold 1995)

The author of this quote, the NHS Director of Human Resources, an NHS manager of long experience, felt compelled to recognize the division that had seemingly emerged between management and operational staff – the doctors, nurses and other professions who deliver patient care. On the same day the Labour MP Alan Milburn, received an answer to his question concerning the administrative costs for health authorities and family health service authorities in England and Wales. The figures showed that costs rose from £775.4 million in 1991–2, the first year of the NHS market, to just over £1 billion in 1993–4. Mr Milburn said the average increase of almost 35 per cent 'gives the lie to government claims that ministers have tackled NHS red tape' (*The Guardian*, 6 June 1995). Thirteen years on from the launch of the 1983 Management Inquiry many of the same issues are still arising. In 1996, the NHS is also a more fractious place to work in. More positively changes set in motion by the 1990 Act may be reaching maturity and a different organizational agenda for change is set to become dominant. Electoral change may play a part in the outcome of the internal market-based reforms but already an opportunity

exists for the medical profession to assert its strength in relation to organizational issues in a period where the will to defend the internal market
and NHS management in general is slipping.

Of key importance is the profession's inclination to act assertively in
relation to management change. It can be argued that while enjoying a
renowned reputation for clinical invention, doctors in the NHS are in
equal measures conservative when it comes to their part in the management process. At the end of a century of extraordinary advances in medical
knowledge, doctors are beginning to acknowledge the need to think crea-
tively in management terms if new clinical services are to be made available to the public. Above the level of the practice, the 'firm' or clinical
team there is little tradition for doctors to draw on when it comes to
participating in organizational innovation. Previous chapters have explored
the remoteness of doctors from strategic levels of management, their partial involvement with the internal market, their ability to avoid changes
implied by the creation of clinical directors and their professional indifference or defensiveness in relation to performance management. In this final
chapter issues surrounding innovation are explored with particular reference paid to the US health care system and its ability to involve doctors
directly in the management of change.

The dead hand of tradition meets the internal market

In the UK, conservatism is written into the profession's constitution in the
form of the primary-secondary care division. Even the profession's choice of
titles seems to be symbolic of a basic antipathy to change. In the USA, the
title commonly accorded to all qualified members of the medical profession
is physician. In Britain however, the term physician has traditionally been
claimed by the doctors who practice in hospitals. The primary-secondary
division was an established feature of the profession by the time the state
established a medical register in 1858. The division originally signifying
class distinctions between the upper middle-class physicians, their less
socially distinguished competitors in surgery, and the apothecaries, themselves originally descendants of grocers who took their income from dis-
pensing drugs. The physicians were educated in the ancient universities,
surgeons and apothecaries undergoing an apprenticeship type of training.
GPs are the descendants of the apothecaries (Hoginsbaum 1979: 1–5).
While the health services underwent major changes between 1858 and
1996, the class distinction remained. The creation of the NHS in 1948
actually built on the division, enshrining the GP-specialist relationship in
the administrative separation of primary and secondary care and through
the referral system.

The division could be claimed to be consistent with standard business
practice in an earlier era. For example the 'functional specialism', denoted
by the separation of GPs and specialists may be seen as consistent with
thinking on how large organizations should organize their employees into

departments such as research and development, production, finance and so on. The GP-specialist division also fitted with the general view that big organizations are more efficient than small organizations. The development of district general hospitals (now trusts) on their present scale was made possible by the act of dividing primary and secondary health care. Relationships between GPs and their colleagues have on certain occasions been strained and are often based on a thin set of formal interactions (Roland 1992).

The internal market, as argued in Chapter 3, may be driving yet another wedge between the two sides of the profession, pitting one group against the other in the struggle for resources. The internal market as constituted, is far from resolving the historic problem created by the sharp distinction made between the practice of primary and secondary care in the NHS. Professional politics still predicate against certain organizational forms, particularly where these involve the destruction of primary-secondary care distinctions. The social class purpose of the division is surely redundant in the 1990s. The medical purpose of a rigid distinction between sectors is questionable. What is certain is that the division presents a very solid obstacle in the way of innovation in service delivery. As a catalyst for change, Working for Patients has made less of a behavioural impact than can be admitted either by government or opposition political parties.

The unwillingness displayed by the medical profession in grasping control of the redesign of the health care system in the UK may mean that leadership is conceded to those with no genuine commitment to innovation. The evidence of management-led 'change activity' is not encouraging.

During 1993–4 the NHS suffered from a 'merger mania'. In England there were amalgamations between regions, district health authorities, family health service authorities and provider units. The Functions and Manpower Review established the basis for mergers at regional level and sanctioned similar activity lower down the hierarchy. Mergers, to quote the chief executive of Guy's and St Thomas' Trust, 'consume huge amounts of management time and resources. The pressures are voracious – and can be very destructive personally' (Garside and Rice 1994). However, the pressures on managers to move their organizations in some positive direction are equally powerful. Senior NHS managers seem frequently to work over sixty hours a week. Managers have to be seen as proactive change agents if they are to be in a position to claim 'successes'. In the highly charged atmosphere of NHS management, where chief executives are hired and fired on a regular basis, rarely is there time for a manager to demonstrate the impact of his or her actions in health outcome terms. By way of compensation, it pays to be seen as leading something highly visible like a merger which has lots of stages to be reached, obstacles to be cleared, and which provides a clear 'outcome target'.

In Hungary in 1948 experiments were carried out on the behavioural responses of pigeons who were being fed a small amount of food every 15 seconds. Apparently the birds sought to identify some connection between their actions and the appearance of food. No such connection existed but the birds would develop fidgeting movements, like feet shuffling or head moving, which they would then convince themselves were responsible for the appearance of the food. In an amusing article, Whitby (1994) a clinical psychologist, suggests that much of what passes for purposive management activity in the NHS is in fact a variation on the same syndrome. At different levels in the NHS, managers are embarking on programmes convinced of their necessity through a process of 'assumed usefulness'. The reality is that professional leadership provided by doctors is not being used properly in the change process. The health care reforms have created a sense of mistrust over the role of politicians in the leadership of the NHS. Kindig and colleagues (1991) note the increasingly prominent management role being taken by physicians in US health care organizations. It is recognized that the US health care system is increasingly organizationally and socially complex and requires a medical input at executive level in order to strike a balance between health care as a 'social good and health care as an economic good'. In the UK, too, a major commitment is required by the medical profession at all levels to rectify a crisis in governance. The public should expect a quality health service provision designed to use available resources both efficiently and effectively. Without medical leadership, 'innovations' are either designed to have no visible impact on clinical services or alternatively are widely interpreted as crude cost cutting exercises. Exposed to a largely suspicious public with increasingly less protection from politicians, NHS managers may be unable to push forward meaningful changes. The Thatcherite 'strong state' of the 1980s gave way to a period of prolonged political uncertainty in the 1990s. Political leadership in health policy became more and more muted.

Managed care lessons from the USA

In comparison to health services in the UK, the US health care system is changing very rapidly. In few other aspects is change more evident than in the relationship of doctors to the management process. It is worth while considering the reasons behind the contrasting experience of reforming this medical management process. Perhaps of crucial significance is the fact that change in the USA is driven by the 'invisible hand' of market forces, while in Britain politicians have been attempting to lead change. In the USA during the 1980s, government and insurers attempted to slow the rate of growth in health care expenditure through resort to resource use restraints such as diagnostic related groups and relative value scales (see Chapter 5). The changes that have taken place in the 1990s have had a more visible impact on the process of clinical care. Commercial logic in the USA is challenging the hospital's position as the traditional base for medicine (Chan 1993). Hospitals were able to expand opportunities for profit during the 1960s and 1970s as the Medicare programme expanded.

(Medicaid and Medicare rose from $3.5 billion to $53.7 billion 1960–78.) During the 1980s the federal government, along with employers and insurers, has been attempting to cap expenditure on health care, pushing the medical industrial corporations into a recessionary situation for the first time. At least some of the medical management technologies, which are currently being experimented with in the NHS, have their origins in the US health care system of the 1980s.

At the beginning of the 1980s, 90 per cent of working Americans gained access to health care through 'indemnity' insurance plans which left them free to choose the physician of their choice. The medical profession was largely unconstrained by regulations curbing their use of particular clinical treatments for financial reasons. The federal government-funded Medicare programme had expanded rapidly since its inception in the mid-1960s and gave patients access to health care on broadly similar lines to private health insurance. Private insurance companies managed both the employer and state purchased health plans and in spite of inflationary costs, adopted a fairly passive position in relation to treatments selected by physicians. Employers and government found that health insurance was spiralling out of control and began to look for ways of limiting expenditure (Moran and Wood 1993; Ham *et al.* 1990). In health care systems like Britain's it is relatively easy for government to limit global spending through budgetary control. In the USA expenditure is theoretically limitless. American health service analysts, while recognizing the institutional structure was not designed to promote cost containment, counter with the argument that success in lump-sum global cost containment is not synonymous with efficiency in delivering health care. These analysts also argue that budget ceilings can adversely impose constraints on the evolutionary development of the health care system in response to technical, scientific and management breakthroughs (Thompson 1992).

The insurance-based system, while unable to impose global budget ceilings, has enjoyed at least partial success in controlling health expenditure since the 1980s (Scheiber *et al.* 1992). Resource management devices such as the diagnostic related group system of limiting a physician's freedom on the course of investigation and treatment offered to a patient, were perhaps relatively easier to introduce in the USA where there is a tradition of fee schedules and tariffs which does not exist in the UK outside the small private sector (Donaldson and Magnussen 1992). The insurers have gradually reined physicians into a more complex structure in which their freedom to investigate and carry out procedures has been by UK standards quite dramatically constrained. While not producing the culture shock such controls would cause in the UK medical profession, the insurer-led initiatives have curtailed freedom and also caused a great deal of administrative work for physicians in independent practice. This has made doctors more interested in changing the organizational context in which they work.

Another pertinent factor in explaining change in the US health care system is that hospitals in the US are no longer free to expand the use of plant and employ new medical technologies. Instead they have been attempting to make profits or expand not-for-profit activity in new free-standing single-purpose centres such as surgicentres, wellness centres, childbirth centres, hemo-dialysis centres. In addition, this type of centre has attracted new investment from outside the traditional hospital base. Hospitals themselves are being bought up by investor-owned chains. The insurers and employers support the development of centres where costs are lower and consumer satisfaction higher. A strong momentum for change has been created. The traditional delivery setting no longer suits evolving health care practice or meets new corporate and consumer demands (Annandale 1989).

The impact that resource management devices launched by insurers and government can make is limited, and the real driving force for change has been the creation of 'managed care organizations'. Managed care is an umbrella term covering a wide range of schemes whereby employers or individuals enrol in a prepaid scheme which guarantees access to health care from a designated list of providers. As a measure of the impact made by managed care organizations it is worth noting that in areas of the USA where there are relatively low percentages of people enrolled in managed care plans, hospitalization rates can be twice as high as in California where health maintenance organizations (HMOs) are well established. Critics argue that this is offset by higher outpatient costs (Finkel 1993).

> Managed care is basically an approach that superimposes organisa-
> tional structure, control, measurement and accountability upon the
> health care system to effect a balance in the utilisation of health care
> resources, cost containment, and quality enhancement. It does so by
> employing three strategies:
> 1 the alteration of financial incentives for providers;
> 2 the introduction of management control; and
> 3 the use of information systems to facilitate operational decisions.
> (Ottensmeyer and Key 1991: 21)

By 1994 over half population in the USA gained access to health services through managed care providers. (The figure was 5 per cent in 1980; Eckholm 1994.) The patient therefore concedes the right to choose their own physician once they enrol in a prepaid scheme.

The managed care organizations are usually called either an HMO or a PPO (preferred provider organization). HMOs make their profits through their ability to manage patient care as a process. Sometimes they are referred to as 'vertically integrated providers', meaning that they manage a patient's whole experience of care from point of first appointment through to specialist treatment and aftercare. Their core business is medical management. They may employ their own doctors or have contracts with a list of doctors working privately on a capitation fee basis. Some HMOs will use a mixture of both. The PPOs are classic network organizations, linked providers who can offer purchasers reduced fees in return for referrals (Chan 1993). Again the PPO essentially makes its money by managing doctors.

HMOs are licensed under the Public Health Service Act. Often HMOs have been founded by doctors. The chief executive of an HMO may or may not be a doctor. The medical director, however, is always a key figure in the organization with control over medical management costs which will be around 85 per cent of the managed care plan's total costs (Ottensmeyer and Key 1991: 22). The skills needed by medical directors are wide. Roles may, for example, include developing a utilization analysis system, constructing an external provider system, finding innovative methods for payment of specialists. Medical directors must also devote energy to establishing favourable contracts for hospital services, where major payoffs can be made. The director of one HMO, formerly a family doctor, defined his role as a type of 'craftsmanship' – keeping information and delivering it where appropriate. He gave the example of an internal medicine specialist whose cardiology work was costing a lot. The HMO's staff reviewed each cardiology referral, comparing this individual's work with colleagues'. An HMO manager saw the specialist and after agreements were made, costs were reduced by 50–60 per cent. This is the economic leverage that a primary care organization can make. They have to be vigilant – to break even requires that they work effectively.

According to the same chief executive, HMOs who employ doctors (referred to as the 'staff model' HMO) must concentrate on hiring policies selecting doctors who can be trained in quality management systems and who can work with colleagues in teams. Doctors who were used to inflating charges in private practice have often been found wanting. Doctors employed by HMOs will usually have an element of their salary paid on the basis of resource utilization and quality measurements which might include:

- response to patient satisfaction surveys
- case by case patient chart review – performance against protocols
- compliance to the HMO's strategic plan.

Clearly, these types of controls are far more proactive than anything that doctors practising in the NHS have experienced. In the USA, not all doctors can adapt to HMO staff conditions. Of the thirty or so doctors on the staff of one HMO in 1990, only a few remained in post four years later.

The more familiar employment relationship in US managed care is conducted through a contractual agreement between self-employed doctors for the care of a patient list provided by the HMO. In one HMO operating on this basis a director described the provider contract as being formatted in a 'you will follow' style. It was really a manual outlining user prices, contractual issues, billing and utilization. The same interviewee acknowledged that the physicians did not actually read the contract/manual, so there had to be a continual round of meetings – gentle 'dinner meetings' and more direct 'focus' and 'satisfaction' meetings. As with staff model HMOs, quality and utilization review for income setting purposes is used to control performance. Quality assurance problems were said by the interviewee to come about infrequently. He liked to maintain an informal relationship where he could cajole and 'advise' rather than invoking a slow, cumbersome sanctions procedure. If there was a special reason for a utilization review he would let the physician discuss it with him. Utilization reviews tend to be conducted by registered nurses. They collect data that is then 'plugged' into systems that measure individual figures against national standards. If there is a serious deviation they approach the physician almost immediately. The spokesman claimed there was no opposition generated over clinical freedom. As far as he was concerned the physicians had signed away clinical freedom. It was his job to make it in the physician's best interests to 'play by the book'. The aim of HMOs is to tie doctors into capitation fee based incomes. A doctor might conceivably work for several HMOs.

Managed care organizations, through resort to more cost effective monitoring and analysis, are able to combine physician's financial profiles with various quality of care indicators based on standardized measures of patient health status, satisfaction surveys and process of care indicators. The records produced at patient and aggregate patient list level are an important factor in marketing the managed care scheme to corporate and individual purchasers of plans (Feinglass and Salmon 1990: 243).

Organizational innovation

On the face of it the US health care system is complicated almost beyond belief. Weiner and Lissovoy (1993), surveying the variants on the managed care theme, counted roughly twenty different organizational entities all involved in providing managed care. These included:

CMP   (Competitive medical plan)
EPO   (Exclusive provider organization)
HIO   (Health insuring organization)
HMO   (Health maintenance organization) (about six varieties)
IPA   (Independent Practice Association)
MSH   (Medical Staff and Hospital)
MIP   (Managed Indemnity Plan)
POS   (Point of Service Plan)
PPA   (Preferred provider arrangement)
PPO   (Preferred provider organization)
R/EPO (Risk sharing exclusive provider organization)
TPA   (Third party administrator)
TOP   (Triple option plan)

They note that critics derisively refer to the 'unintelligible alphabet soup of three letter health plans'. To make matters even less clear the managed care organizations interact continually through contractual agreements to form a highly complex web of relationships. Yet from a patient's perspective the relationship with the managed care organization and its doctors is normally straightforward. In spite of the organizational complexity, or perhaps more to the point because of it, the patient receives 'a seamless product' (Weiner and Lissovoy 1993). A feature of many managed care packages used for marketing purposes is the ease of access and absence of billing involved for the patient.

The managed care organizations have an incentive to provide services of the type and price that the insurers, employers and patients want and attempt to create the network relationships needed to achieve this (Johnston and Lawrence 1988). As the agents in charge of both primary and secondary health care for their patients they have been influential in creating new non-hospital institutions. The traditional hospitals also have to provide the services that the managed care organizations think are appropriate. The insurers and employers support the development of centres where costs are lower and consumer satisfaction higher. A strong drive for decentralization has been created. The significance of the proliferation of managed care organizations in the USA, from a British point of view, is in the ability of the US system to involve doctors in creating different means of combining organization, finance and medical practice. By comparison, the NHS internal market seems unable to provide the stimulus for this entrepreneurial process to take place.

Impact on the profession in the USA

An inherently conservative medical profession based in the NHS may be witnessing events in the USA with growing discomfort, alternatively in some cases envy. The implications for the US medical profession of organizational change have been scrutinized closely. In the 1970s, there was a growing awareness that the medical profession were in some form of retreat as a power. A radical North American literature built up around the themes of 'proletarianization', 'de-professionalization' and 'loss of dominance' in hospitals. The 'de-professionalization' school argued that medical work was being increasingly ensnared in rules and structures designed to realize the maximum return for private capital. McKinlay and Stoakle (1988: 200) refer to the 'corporate purchase' of the health care profession in the USA. The profession, they argue, has been 'divested of control over certain key prerogatives relating to the location, content and essentiality of its task activities'. Managers are seen as incorporating doctors into a medical team, composed of various practitioners from medical and related backgrounds. This is said to be stripping physicians of power formerly exercised as individuals. An oversupply of practitioners is seen as strengthening the corporate buy up of the medical profession. There is a flight of physicians in the USA away from independent practice where they charge on a fee-for-service basis into organizational contexts which vary considerably around a managed care theme, but where clinical decisions are always the subject of controls (Fry *et al.* 1995: 100).

However, the loss of medical power incurred as a result of change in the US health care system may be exaggerated. Friedson (1986: 63–79) argues that doctors have not lost out at the 'macro-level' where professional bodies are still exercising control over members' regulation and codification credentialling and discipline. At the meso or institutional/organizational level change is occurring, though not in one direction. Frequently, doctors are assuming more important management roles in HMOs and hospitals (Alpander and Strong 1991). However, at the micro level Friedson sees a process of stratification taking place where elites based on knowledge, administrative power and disciplinary authority are emerging along with a large rank and file bearing the brunt of increased surveillance and evaluation.

Inevitably the profession will become stratified into an elite and rank and file. Friedson predicts 'the collapse of norms governing the way colleagues evaluate and control each other'. He gives the causes as an increase in malpractice suits and federal/state attempts to control expenditure. Professional disciplinary boards and licensing boards are also more active. Some states effectively force doctors to report gross negligence of their colleagues. Medical work is being evaluated far more heavily than in previous times. Patients' rights have become the focus for legal reform. Computer protocols limit autonomy but these controls are created by a physician elite, and reinforced by an administrative elite. The rank and file, though still a profession with some meaningful degree of autonomy, are now more constrained by norms laid down by a select group of their own colleagues (Coburn 1992: 497–512). The lesson would seem to be that organizational change is an opportunity for some physicians to influence events more strategically than previously and the creation of new regulatory roles for others, with mixed consequences for the working conditions of the rest. The lesson would appear to be that the medical profession in the USA is capable of considerable adaptiveness in response to new challenges.

Explaining inertia in the UK

If expenditure control, organizational and clinical innovation are all part of an integrated change process in the USA, by contrast, organizational change in the NHS seems to have separated clinical developments from the politically driven internal market reforms. Physicians in the UK have, over the past decade, become ensnared in a mind set where the starting rationale for reform of all public services is derived from a managerialist ideology. This has been translated into practice through recycled business devices such as performance indicators, short-term contracts, performance related pay and a familiar pattern of organizational restructuring based on devolving budgets, quasi-markets and privatization (Harrison *et al.* 1992: 118--48).

The reforms carried an implicit assumption that organizational change would take place to facilitate the development of new health care delivery systems. In reality 'entrepreneurial activity' has been confined largely to the domain of the general manager, consisting of health authority mergers and re-designs of existing organizations rather than the provision of innovative forms of delivering health services. The NHS Management Executive recently published a guide to the 'operation of the internal market', 50 per cent of which is devoted to the subject of provider mergers and 'joint ventures', and purchaser mergers and boundary adjustments. The remaining 50 per cent of the guide deals with 'providers in difficulty' and 'collusive behaviour'. Service delivery innovation is nowhere mentioned (NHS Executive 1994). The internal market, coupled as it is to a managerialist mindset, may well be seen in the future as having extended the life of clinically outdated practices and institutions in the NHS.

Innovation and entrepreneurship

The business of innovation appears to be poorly conceived in the NHS of the 1990s. The internal market might initially be seen as creating the 'right' environment for innovation to take place in. However, the evidence of the first five years fails to indicate that doctors are being given the right signals from either the internal market, their employers in the trusts or by central government to pursue creative ideas for the provision of health services. The entrepreneurial process involves 'the functions, activities and actions associated with the perceiving of opportunities and the creation of organizations to pursue them' (Bygrave and Hofer 1991). Explanations for the stimulation of entrepreneurial action fall into three basic categories. The first stresses the individual and 'personological traits' such as the entrepreneur's unusually high need for achievement, challenges, independence and risk-taking (McClelland 1961). A variant on the same theme draws attention to the allegedly deviant psychological disposition of the entrepreneur – a misfit who fails to function in a conventional employee role (Kets de Vries 1977). A second discernible school of thought attempts to link entrepreneurial behaviour to 'situational' variables such as class, education and training (Gibb and Ritchie 1981). The third category of explanation relies on a behavioural analysis which concentrates on the activities undertaken to enable organizations to come into existence (Gartner 1989).

The situational and behavioural approaches offer the more fruitful source of ideas for identifying the strengths and weaknesses of the US and UK medical profession in relation to innovative behaviour. The behaviouralist view places the organization at the centre of an 'entrepreneurial event' that takes place in pursuit of a new opportunity. A multitude of factors are involved in this event, causality may be impossible to identify. Nevertheless, we may say with certainty that the US health care system is evidently more prone to entrepreneurial behaviour than the NHS.

The entrepreneurial opportunities available to doctors in the USA are considerable. Based on interviews with a large number of doctors in the

1990s, Johnson (1992) explored the range of perceived opportunities opening up. The resulting article uses the device of a fictional character pondering which direction to take at a crossroads in his career as a solo practitioner. With more boring paperwork, the need for capital investment in the practice, longer hours and a declining income, solo practice has become less attractive, and the possibilities are reviewed. The option of applying for a medical director's post in a hospital was quickly dismissed as not attractive to someone with many years experience of 'being his own boss'. More promisingly, professional colleagues were openly discussing various 'joint ventures', involving individual investments and a bank loan to set up a surgical centre for out-patients. The business plan was convincing. There were many other possibilities for joint ventures with other doctors. Johnson's character could envisage getting involved in, for example, a stress laboratory, an executive physical examination programme, an industrial medicine programme, a pharmacy. A less risky possibility was simply to take a job with a hospital or staff model HMO. Alternatively, there was the option of greatly expanding the limited set of contracts he held with managed care organizations. Working for managed care organizations was all about balancing economic decisions with the clinical interests of each patient. The draw-backs of managed care, Johnson concluded, were outweighed for him personally by the advantages. As a 'managed care entrepreneur' he would make his reward through his ability to use specialists judiciously, closely monitoring the hospital days needed by his patients, using the most cost-effective hospital. Having learned how to manage patient care in this context, he would then employ four newly primary care qualified physicians.

Replicating these career opportunities within the context of a publicly financed NHS is not possible in the mid-1990s. Perhaps it is professional training and socialization that is the key factor. This has, after all, for several generations, taken place within a state owned monopoly and may be the reason for the lack of inclination towards innovation. The Thatcher decade may also have produced a climate of fear in the welfare state, causing the doctors to cling onto 'traditional' institutions which become sources of comfort. Alternatively, the existing pricing and contract system may discourage entrepreneurial behaviour.

The need to take the lead

The medical profession in the UK face an increasingly uncomfortable future under the current NHS management regime. It can be argued that the NHS was, for the first forty years of its existence, controlled through a delicate mixture of hierarchy and forms of regulation based on negotiation between the state and semi-autonomous professional groups. Political rhetoric suggests the NHS is supposed to become part of a responsive or supermarket state which is driven along by consumer preferences, while evidence of actual change leads to the conclusion that progress is being made in the direction of greater hierarchy. Global budget controls have always been an important element in the NHS but over the past decade these have been steadily supplemented by budgetary control, devices which are now increasingly being targeted to ensnare doctors. Peer group control and socialization is likely to remain highly important in medicine but will be conducted *within* a predominantly hierarchical regime that is driven by financial measures and controls. A pact is likely whereby professional standards, though remaining under the control of an autonomous professional body, increasingly will be reconciled with strict financial control.

Paradoxically, this may prove less of a shock to the medical profession than might be anticipated. The medical profession, though increasingly forced to take on a managerialist role, may find that this is an accommodation which is palatable. The alternative of an entrepreneurial role may be much more difficult to stomach, given that it implies the destruction of the basic structure (the primary–secondary split) through which medicine is practised in Britain. Innovation necessarily challenges traditional power relationships and cultural norms. The challenge may be avoided by a defensive, conservative profession preferring to pay the price of becoming the implementors of finance-based controls in return for the right to maintain control of medical standards, education and socialization.

If it is to assume a proactive, shaping role in the changing organization of health services the medical profession must be prepared to examine its role in relation to the governance of the NHS. Governance is, according to Sheridan and Kendall (1992), concerned with the highest echelons of an organization, and separate from management. It is concerned with directing and controlling lower levels and influencing behaviour throughout the organization. Governance is, by definition, strategic in nature, but is not to be confused with simple concepts of directive 'leadership' since there should be a clear understanding of how stakeholders' interests are to be reconciled in corporate terms that can be translated into organizational practice.

In the context of the NHS it is essential that the medical profession participate fully in the governance of health services provision. Given the new clinical practice opportunities that are emerging, increasingly the governance role will demand a mixture of professional expertise and professional risk taking in establishing new health care organizational practice within the NHS, or in a networked relationship with the NHS. The medical profession cannot rely on being able to influence health service provision in the future if it maintains a 'caretaker mentality' (Shortell: 1989). Only the medical profession can inform the governance of the NHS with sufficient confidence to develop a strategy that both exploits innovative practice and maintains a balance between the stakeholder interests of patients, NHS staff and wider society. This involves a re-invention of the relationship between the profession and the management process.

References

Acheson, D. (1991) 'The Health Service Commissioner', *Health Trends*, 50(1): 61–3.

Alpander, G. (1991) 'A perceptual study of the role of the staff president of the medical staff', *Hospital and Health Services Administration*, 36(2): 271–83.

Alvesson, M. and Lindkvist, L. (1993) 'Transaction costs, clans and corporate culture', *Journal of Management Studies*, 30(3): 427–52.

Annandale, E. (1989) 'Proletarianization or restratification of the medical profession?', *International Journal of Health Services*, 19(4): 611–34.

Appleby, J., Smith, P., Ranade, W., Little, V., and Robinson, R. (ed.) (1993) 'Competition and the NHS', in I. Tilley, *Managing the Internal Market*. London, Paul Chapman.

Appleby, J., Smith, P., Ranade, W., Little, V., and Robinson, R. (1994) 'Monitoring managed competition', in R. Robinson and J. Le Grand (eds), *Evaluating the NHS Reforms*. London, Kings Fund Institute.

Ashburner, L. and Cairncross, L. (1993) 'Membership of the new style health authorities: continuity or change?', *Public Administration*, 71(3): 357–75.

Audit Commission (1995) *The Doctors' Tale*, London, HMSO.

Baeza, J., Tilley, I. and Salt, D. (1993) 'Contracts, budgets and workloads: understanding power and influence in NHS hospitals.' Paper presented to Conference on Professions and Management in Britain, University of Stirling.

Baggot, R. (1994) *Health and Health Care in Britain*. London, Macmillan.

Baker, M. (1994) 'The role of medical directors in Trusts', in M. Burrows *et al.*, *Management for Doctors*. Oxford, Butterworth Heinemann.

Barker, P. (1990) 'The Leicester experience', *Health Services Journal*, 27 September: 1428–9.

Bartlett, W. and Le Grand, J. (1994) 'The Performance of Trusts', in R. Robinson and J. Le Grand (eds), *Evaluating the NHS Reforms*. London, Kings Fund.

Beale, V. and Pollitt, C. (1994) 'Charters at the grass roots: a First Report', *Local Government Studies*, 20(2): 202–25.

British Medical Association (BMA) (1990) *Guidance on Clinical Directorates.* London, BMA.

Boufford, J. (1994) *Shifting the Balance from Acute to Community Health Care.* London, Kings Fund.

Bowie, C. and Harris, T. (1994) 'The fundholding fandango', *British Journal of General Practice*, 44–5: 38–40.

British Journal of Nursing (1994), 3(9): 6.

British Medical Journal (1993), 306: 1017–18.

Bulivant, J. and Naylor, M. (1992) 'Best of the best', *Health Service Journal*, 27 August.

Burgoyne, J. and Lorbiecki, A. (1993) 'Clinicians into management', *Health Services Management Research*, 6(4).

Burrows, M., Dyson, R., Jackson, P. and Saxton, H. (1994) *Management for Doctors.* Oxford, Butterworth Heinemann.

Buxton, M., Packwood, T. and Keen, J. (1991) *Final Report of the Brunel University Evaluation of Resource Management.* Uxbridge, Brunel University.

Bygrave, D. and Hofer, C. (1991) 'Theorising about entrepreneurship', *Entrepreneurship Theory and Practice*, 16(2): 2–20.

Campling, E., Devlin, H., Hoile, R. and Lunn, J. (1993) *The Report of the National Confidential Enquiry into Perioperative Deaths 1991/92.* London, NCEPOD.

Capewell, S. (1992) 'Clinical directorates: a panacea for clinicians involved in management?', *Health Bulletin*, 50(6): 441–7.

Capewell, S. (1994) 'What users think: a survey of NHS users in Scotland in 1992', *Health Bulletin*, 52(1): 26–34.

Carter, N. (1991) 'Learning to measure performance', *Public Administration*, 69(1): 85–102.

Chan, P. (1993) 'The Strategic Restructuring of US Hospitals', *Journal of Management in Medicine*, 7(1).

Chan, P. (1993) 'The Strategic Restructuring of US Hospitals', *Journal of Management in Medicine*, 7(1): 47–56.

Chantler, C. (1993) 'Historical background: where have clinical directorates come from and what is their purpose?', in A. Hopkins (ed.), *The Role of Hospital Consultants in Clinical Directorates. The Synchromesh Report.* London, Royal College of Physicians.

Clarke, J., Cochrane, A. and McLaughlin, E. (1994) *Managing Social Policy.* London, Sage.

Cluzeau, F., Littlejohns, P. and Grimshaw, J. (1994) 'Appraising clinical guidelines: towards a "Which" guide for purchasers', *Quality in Health Care*, 3(3): 121–2.

Coburn, D. (1992) 'Friedson then and now. An internalist critique of Friedson's past and present views of the medical profession', *International Journal of Health Services*, 22(3): 381–96.

Cohen, P. (1994) 'Patient's Charter: passing the buck?', *Nursing Times*, 90(13): 28–30.

Costain, D. (ed.) (1990) *The Future of Acute Services: Doctors as Managers.* London, Kings Fund.

Crail, M. (1994) 'Blinking Indicators', *Health Service Journal*, 4: 10–11.

Davis, C. and Rhodes, D. (1988) 'The impact of DRGs on the cost and quality of health care in the United States', *Health Policy*, 9: 117–31.

Dearden, B. (1991) 'Shaping doctors to organisations or organisations to doctors', *Journal of Management in Medicine*, 5(1).

Deming, W. (1988) *Out of the Crisis*. Cambridge, Mass., MIT Press.

Denzin, N. (1970) *The Research Act in Sociology*. London, Butterworth.

Department of Health (1986) *The Health of the Nation*. London, HMSO.

Department of Health (1990) *Medical Audit in Family Practitioner Services* (Health circular) (FP (90) 8). London, HMSO.

Department of Health (1991) *The Patient's Charter*. London, HMSO.

Department of Health and Social Security (DHSS) (1972) *National Health Service Reorganisation: England*, Cmnd 5055. London, HMSO.

Department of Health and Social Security (DHSS) (1983) 'NHS Management Inquiry', Press Release No. 83/30, 3 February.

Department of Health and Social Security (DHSS) (1986) *Health Service Management Resource Management (Management Budgeting) in Health Authorities* (HN (86) 34). London, HMSO.

Department of Health, *Medical Audit in Family Practitioner Services* (HC (FP) (90) (8)). London, HMSO.

Department of Health, Welsh Office and Scottish Home and Health Department (1989a) *Working for Patients*, Cm 5555. London, HMSO.

Department of Health, Welsh Office and Scottish Home and Health Department (1989b) *Working for Patients Working Paper 3 Practice Budgets for General Medical Practitioners*, Cm 5555. London, HMSO.

Department of Health, Welsh Office and Scottish Home and Health Department (1989c) *Working for Patients Working Paper 2 Self Governing Hospitals*, Cm 5555. London, HMSO.

Department of Health (1989d) *Working for Patients: Medical Audit Working Paper 6*. London, HMSO.

Department of Health (1990) *National Health Service and Community Care Act 1990*. London, HMSO.

Disken, S., Dixon, M., Halpern, S. and Shocket, G. (1990) *Models of Clinical Management*. London, IHSM.

Donaldson, C. and Magnussen, J. (1992) 'DRGs: the road to hospital efficiency', *Health Policy*, 21: 47–64.

Donaldson, L., Kirkup, W., Craig, N. and Parkin, D. (1994) 'Lanterns in the jungle: is the NHS driven by the wrong kind of efficiency?', *Public Health*, 108: 2–9.

Dopson, S. (1993) 'Management the one disease consultants did not think existed.' Paper presented to Conference on Professions and Management in Britain, University of Stirling.

Dougherty, D. and Bowman, E. (1995) 'The effects of organizational downsizing on product innovation', *California Management Review*, 37(4): 28–44.

Dowd, B., Christianson, J., Feldman, R., Wisner, C. and Klein, J. (1992) 'Issues regarding health plan payments under medicare and recommendations for reform', *Milbank Quarterly*, 70(3): 423–53.

Drewry, G. and Butcher, T. (1988) *The Civil Service Today*. Oxford, Basil Blackwell.

Drucker, P. (1988) 'The coming of new organisations', *Harvard Business Review*, 66(1): 56–9.

Drucker, P. (1992) *Post-Capitalist Society*. London, Harper Business.

Eckholm, E. (1994) *New York Times*, 12 December.

Feinglass, J. and Salmon, W. (1990) 'Corporatization of medicine', *International Journal of Health Services*, 20(2): 23–52.

Ferlie, E. and Pettigrew, A. (1995) 'Managing Through Networks: Some Implications for the NHS'. British Academy of Management Annual Conference.

Ferlie, E., Fitzgerald, L. and Ashburner, L. (1992) *Boards and the New Health Authorities; The Challenge of Purchasing*. Centre for Corporate Strategy, University of Warwick.

Ferlie, E., Ashburner, L. and Fitzgerald, L. (1994) *Corporate Governance and the Public Sector*. Centre for Corporate Strategy and Change, Warwick Business School.

Finkel, M. (1993) 'Managed care is not the answer', *Journal of Health Politics and Law*, 18(1): 106–12.

Fisher, N., Smith, H. and Pasternak, D. (1993) 'Critical factors in recruiting health maintenance organization physicians', *Health Care Management Review*, 18(1): 51–61.

Fitzgerald, L. (1991) This Year's Model, *Health Service Journal*, 7 November.

Fitzgerald, L. (1992) *Management Development for Consultants: Formative Evaluation of the Doctors in Business Schools Programme. Final Report*. Centre for Corporate Strategy and Change, Warwick Business School.

Fitzgerald, L. and Stuart, J. (1992) 'Clinicians in to management: on the change agenda or not?', *Health Services Management Research*, 5(2).

Fogel, D. (1989) 'The uniqueness of a professionally dominated organisation', *Health Care Management Review*, 14(3): 15–24.

Friedman, M. (1976) *Price Theory: A Provisional Text*. Chicago, Aldine.

Friedson, E. (1986) 'The medical profession in transition', in L. Aiken and D. Mechanic (eds), *Applications of Social Science to Clinical Medicine and Health Policy*. New Jersey, Rutgers University Press.

Frostick, S. and Wallace, W. (1993) 'Mainstream specialisms and the NHS market: the case of surgery', in I. Tilley (ed.), *Managing the Internal Market*. London, Paul Chapman.

Fry, J., Light, D., Rodnick, J. and Orton, P. (1995) *Reviving Primary Care*. Oxford, Radcliffe.

Garside, P. and Rice, J. (1994) 'Merger mania', *Health Service Journal*, 21 July.

Gartner, W. (1989) 'Who is an entrepreneur?', *Entrepreneurship Theory and Practice*, Summer.

General Practitioner (1994) May 13: 1–2.

Gibb, A. and Ritchie, J. (1981) 'Understanding the process of starting small businesses', *European Small Business Journal*, 1(1): 9–17.

Gill, P. (1993) 'Who's Counting?', *Health Service Journal*, 15 April: 27–8.

Glennerster, H., Matsaganis, M. and Owens, P. (1992) *A Foothold for Fundholding*. London, King's Fund Institute.

Glennerster, H., Matsaganis, M., Owens, P. and Hancock, S. (1994) 'GP Fundholding: Wildcard or Winning Hand?', in R. Robinson and J. Le Grand (eds), *Evaluating the NHS Reforms*. London, King's Fund Institute.

Glennerster, H. (1994) 'The future of fundholding', in A. Harrison (ed.), *Health Care UK*, London, Kings Fund Institute.

Glynn, J., Gray, A. and Jenkins, B. (1992) 'Auditing the three Es: the challenge of effectiveness', JUC Public Administration Conference, University of York, 7–9 September: 1–21.

Godt, P. (1987) 'Confrontation, consent, and corporatism: state strategies and the medical profession in France, Great Britain, and West Germany', *Journal of Health Politics, Policy and Law*, 12(3): 459–80.

Goffee, R. and Scase, R. (1995) *Corporate Realities*. London, Routledge.

Gray, A. and Jenkins, W. (1985) *Administrative Politics in British Government*. Brighton, Harvester.

Gray, A. and Jenkins, W. (1991) 'The management of change in Whitehall', *Public Administration*, 69(1): 41–60.

Greatorex, I. and Edgell, C. (1993) 'How can clinical directors influence the purchaser?', *The Clinician in Management*, 2(5): 4–6.

Greenfield, S., Parle, J. and Nayak, A. (1994) 'Practice managers: who are they? What do they do?' Paper presented at BSA Medical Sociology Group 26th Annual Conference, University of York, October.

Grimshaw, J. and Russell, I. (1993) 'Effects of clinical guidelines in medical practice', *The Lancet*, 342.

Ham, C. (1992) *Health Policy in Britain* (3rd edn). London, Macmillan.

Ham, C. and Hill, M. (1984) *The Policy Process in the Capitalist State*. Brighton, Wheatsheaf.

Ham, C. and Hunter, D. (1988) 'Managing clinical activity in the NHS'. Briefing Paper 8. London, Kings Fund Institute.

Ham, C., Robinson, R. and Benzeval, M. (1990) *Health Check: Health Care Reforms in an International Context*. London, Kings Fund Institute.

Handy, C. (1989) *Age of Unreason*. London, Arrow.

Harrison, S. (1988) *Managing the National Health Service: Shifting the Frontier?* London, Chapman and Hall.

Harrison, S. (1994) *National Health Service Management in the 1980s*. Aldershot, Avebury.

Harrison, S., Hunter, D. and Pollitt, C. (1990) *The Dynamics of British Health Policy*. London, Unwin Hyman.

Harrison, S., Hunter, D., Marnoch, G. and Pollitt, C. (1989) 'General management and medical autonomy in the National Health Service', *Health Services Management Research* 2(1): 38–46.

Harrison, S., Hunter, D., Marnoch, G. and Pollitt, C. (1992) *Just Managing: Power and Culture in the NHS*. London, Macmillan.

Harvey Jones, J. (1993) *Managing to Survive*. London, Mandarin.

Harwood, A. and Boufford, J. (1993) *Managing Clinical Services. A Consensus Statement of Principles for Effective Clinical Management*. London, BAMM; BMA; IHSM; RCN.

Health Service Journal (1993) 23 September: 5–6.

Health Service Journal/GLAXO (1993) 'Healthy' Debate, *Health Service Journal*, 14 October: 14–15.

Heymann, T. (1994) 'Clinical protocols are key to quality health care delivery', *International Journal of Health Care Quality Assurance*, 7(7): 14–17.

Hogg, C. and Cowl, J. (1994) 'Different strokes', *Health Service Journal*, 12 May: 12–13.

Hoginsbaum, F. (1979) *The Division in British Medicine*. New York, St Martin's Press.

Hogwood, B. and Gunn, L. (1984) *Policy Analysis for the Real World*. Oxford, Oxford University Press.

Hopkins, A. (ed.) *The role of hospital consultants in clinical directorates. The syncromesh report*. London, Royal College of Physicians.

Horton, S. and Farnham, D. (1993) *Managing the New Public Services*. London, Macmillan.

Humphrey, C. and Berrow, D. (1993) 'Developing the role of medical audit advisory groups', *Quality in Health Care*, 2(4): 232–8.

Hunter, D. (1993) *Health Service Journal*, 7 October: 21.

Huxham, C. and Botham, J. (1995) 'Bridging the divide: the duality of roles for medical directors and clinicians in the new NHS', *Public Money and Management*, 15(2): 27–35.

Iles, V., Cramp, D. and Carson, E. (1993) 'Linking clinical reality with strategic management', in M. Malek, J. Rasquinha and P. Vacani (eds), *Strategic Issues in Health Care Management*. Chichester, John Wiley.

Irvine, D. (1993) 'General practice in the 1990s: a personal view on future developments', *British Journal of General Practice*, 43: 121–5.

Jackson, P. (1993) 'Public service performance evaluation: a strategic perspective', *Public Money and Management*, 13(4): 9–14.

Jackson, P. and Saxton, H. *Management for Doctors*. Oxford, Butterworth Heinemann.

Jarrold, K. (1995) *Minding Our Own Business*. Birmingham, NAHAT.

Jenkins, L., Bordsley, M., Coles, J. and Wickings, I. (1988) *How Did We Do? The Use of Performance Indicators in the National Health Service*. London, CASPE Research.

Johnson, R. (1992) 'The entrepreneurial physician', *Health Care Management Review*, 17(1): 73–9.

Johnston, R. and Lawrence, P. (1988) 'Beyond vertical integration – the rise of value-adding partnership', *Harvard Business Review*, July–August: 94–101.

Jones, J. (1994) 'Patients at risk from rookie surgeons', *Sunday Times*, 5 June: 17.

Jones, T. and Prowle, M. (1984) *Health Service Finance: an Introduction*. London, Certified Accountants Educational Trust.

Jorgensen, T. (1993) 'Modes of governance and administrative change', in Kooiman, J. (ed.) *Modern Governance*. London, Sage.

Kellener, P. (1980) 'How Whitehall is learning the lesson of M and S', *Sunday Times*, 24 August.

Kerrison, S., Packwood, T. and Buxton, M. (1993) *Medical Audit: Taking Stock*. London, Kings Fund Centre.

Kets de Vries, M. (1977) 'The entrepreneurial personality: a person at the crossroads', *Journal of Management Studies*, 14(1): 34–57.

Kindig, D., Cross Dunham, N. and Man Chun, L. (1991) 'Career paths of physician executives', *Health Care Management Review*, 16(4): 11–20.

King, M., Lapsley, I., Mitchell, F. and Moyes, J. (1994) 'Costing needs and practices in a changing environment: the potential for ABC in the NHS', *Financial Accountability and Management*, 102: 143–60.

Kingman, S. (1993) 'The Freeman Hospital: disillusionment sets in', *British Medical Journal*, 306: 1464–7.

Kissick, W. (1988) 'The secularization of health affairs', *Hospital and Health Services Administration*, 33(3): 283–95.

Kleefield, S., Churchill, W. and Laffel, G. (1991) 'Improvements in a hospital pharmacy department', *Quality Review Bulletin*, 17: 138–43.

Kogan, M., Henkel, M., Joss, R. and Spink, M. (1991) *Evaluation of Total Quality Management Projects in the National Health Service*. Centre for the Evaluation of Public Policy and Practice, Brunel University.

Kogan, M., Henkel, M., Joss, R. and Balkwill, C. (1992) *Developments at the National Health Service Total Quality Management Demonstration Sites Between July 1991 and July 1992*. Centre for the Evaluation of Public Policy and Practice, Brunel University.

Kooiman, J. (ed.) (1993) *Modern Governance*. London, Sage.

Laing, A. and Cotton, S. (1995) 'Towards an understanding of health care purchasing', *Journal of Marketing Management*, 11: 583–600.

Lapsley, I. (1994) 'Market mechanisms and the management of health care', *International Journal of Public Sector Management*, 7(6): 15–25.

Lawrence, M. and Schofield, T. (eds) (1993) *Medical Audit in Primary Health Care*. Oxford: Oxford University Press.

Lawrence, M. (1993) 'What is audit?', in M. Lawrence and T. Schofield (eds), *Medical Audit in Primary Health Care*. Oxford: Oxford University Press.

Le Grand, J. and Bartlett, W. (1993) *Quasi-Markets and Social Policy*. London, Macmillan.

Levitt, R. and Wall, A. (1992) *The Reorganized National Health Service* (4th ed). London, Chapman and Hall.

Light, D. (1995) *The Future of Fundholding*. London, IHSM.

Likierman, A. (1993) 'Performance indicators: 20 early lessons from managerial use', *Public Money and Management*, October–December: 15–22.

Littler, C. (1985) 'Taylorism, Fordism and job design', in D. Knights, H. Willmott and C. Collinson (eds), *'Job Redesign'*. Aldershot, Gower.

Lorbiecki, A., Snell, R. and Burgoyne, J. (1992) *Final Report of the National Evaluation of the First Wave Management Development Initiative for Hospital Consultants*. Department of Management Learning, Lancaster University.

Lugon, M. and Mills, S. (1994) 'Medical director or agent provocateur', *The Clinician in Management*, 3(1): 12–13.

Mabey, C. and Mayon-White, B. (1993) *Managing Change*. London, Paul Chapman.

MacAlister, L. (1994) 'NHS league tables: does a 5 star rating mean 5 star care', *British Journal of Nursing*, 3(13): 647–8.

MacKerrell, D. (1993) 'Contract pricing: a management opportunity', in I. Tilley (ed.) *Managing the Internal Market*. London, Paul Chapman.

Macmillan, L. and Pringle, M. (1992) 'Practice managers and practice management', *British Medical Journal*, 304: 1672–4.

Mahmood, R. and Chisnell, C. (1993) 'Do doctors want to become involved in management?', *The Clinician in Management*, 2(4): 12–14.

Maidment, R. and Thompson, G. (eds) (1993) *Managing the United Kingdom*. London, Sage.

Marinker, M. (1987) 'Partnership', *Family Practice*, 4(3): 157–9.

Mark, A. (1991) 'Where are the medical managers?', *Journal of Management in Medicine*, 5(4): 6–12.

Marnoch, G., Cotton, S., Laing, A. and Phillips, P. (1996) 'Market structure in health care: geographic determinism in GP's choices of hospitals'. *Rural Scotland and Urban England Compared*. Unpublished paper.

Maynard, A. (1993a) 'Creating competition in the NHS: Is it possible? Will it work?', in I. Tilley (ed.), *Managing the Internal Market*. London, Paul Chapman.

Maynard, A. (1993b) 'The plain truth about doctors', *Health Service Journal*, 19 August: 21.

McKinlay, J. and Arches, J. (1985) 'Towards the proletarianization of physicians', *International Journal of Health Services*, 15: 161–95.

McKinlay, J. and Stoakle, J. (1988) 'Corporatization and the social transformation of doctoring', *International Journal of Health Services*, 118(2): 191–205.

McLelland, D. (1961) *The Achieving Society*. Princeton NJ, Van Nostrand.

Miles, R. and Snow, C. (1986) 'Causes of failure in network organisations', *California Management Review*, 28(3): 62–72.

Miller, F. and Harrison, A. (1993) 'Malpractice liability and physician autonomy', *The Lancet*, 342, 16 October: 973–4.

Ministry of Health (1967) *First Report of the Joint Working Party on the Organisation of Medical Work in Hospitals*, London, HMSO.

Mintzberg, H. (1973) *The Nature of Managerial Work*. New York, Harper and Row.

Mintzberg, H. (1989) *Mintzberg on Management*. New York, New York Free Press.

Mohan, J. (1995) *A National Health Service?* London, Macmillan.

Mole, V. and Dawson, S. (1993) 'Special report on clinical management', *Health Service Journal*, 11 March: 33–4.

Moran, M. (1994) 'Re-shaping the health care state', *Government and Opposition*, 29(1).

Moran, M. and Wood, B. (1993) *Regulation and the Medical Profession*. Buckingham, Open University Press.

Morgan, C. and Murgatroyd, S. (1994) *Total Quality Management in the Public Sector*. Buckingham, Open University Press.

Munro, K. (1993) 'Auditing Teamwork', in M. Lawrence and T. Schofield (eds), *Medical Audit in Primary Health Care*. Oxford, Oxford University Press.

National Health Service in Scotland (1994a) *The Patient's Charter: Raising the Standards in Scotland*. Edinburgh, Scottish Office.

National Health Service in Scotland (1994b), *Clinical Outcome Indicators*. Edinburgh, Scottish Office.

NHS Management Executive – Scottish Home and Health Department (1991) *NHS Trusts: A Working Guide*. Edinburgh, Scottish Office.

National Health Service in Scotland (1991) *The Patient's Charter: Charter for Health*. Edinburgh, Scottish Office.

National Health Service Management Inquiry (1983) *The Griffiths Report*. London, Department of Health and Social Security.

NHS Executive (1994) *The Operation of the NHS Internal Market*. London, Department of Health.

NHS Executive (1995a) Kendell Working Party Report Advance Letter (MD), 6/95 August.

NHS Executive (1995b) Revised Arrangements for B, A and A+ Distinction Awards: Guide to the NHS Consultant's Distinction Award Scheme EL(95)109, October 1995.

OECD (1987) *Financing and Delivering Health Care*. Paris, OECD.

Office of Health Economics (1995) *Compendium of Statistics* (9th edn). HMSO, London.

Oliver, T. (1993) 'Analysis, advice and congressional leadership: the Physician Payment Review Commission and the politics of Medicare', *Journal of Health Politics, Policy and Law*, 18(1): 112–74.

Osborne, D. and Gaebler, T. (1992) *Reinventing Government: How the Entrepreneurial Spirit is Transforming the Public Sector*. Reading, Mass., Addison-Wesley.

Ottensmeyer, D. and Key, M. (1991) 'Lessons learned hiring HMO medical directors', *Health Care Management Review* 16(2): 21–30.

Øvretveit, J. (1992) *Health Service Quality*. Oxford, Blackwell Scientific.

Øvretveit, J. (1990) 'What is quality in health services?', *Health Services Management*, June: 132–3.

Packwood, T., Keen, J. and Buxton, M. (1991) *Hospitals in Transition*. Buckingham, Open University Press.

Painter, C. (1994) 'Public service reform: reinventing or abandoning government', *The Political Quarterly*, 65(3): 242–62.

Pascale, R. (1991) *Managing on the Edge*. London, Penguin.

Peters, T. (1993) *Liberation Management*. London, Pan.

Pettigrew, A., Ferlie, E. and McKee, L. (1992) *Shaping Strategic Change*. London, Sage.

Phelps Brown, H. (1983) *The Origins of Trade Union Power*. Oxford, Clarendon.

Plamping, D. and Fischer, M. (1994) 'Family Values', *Health Service Journal*, 18 August: 22–3.

Pollitt, C. (1990) *Management of Public Services: An Anglo-American Comparison*. London, Basil Blackwell.

Pollitt, C. (1993) 'The politics of medical quality: auditing doctors in the UK and the USA', *Health Services Management Research*, 6(1): 24–34.

Pollitt, C. (1996) 'Business approaches to quality improvement: why they are hard to swallow.' Paper presented University of Aberdeen Health Services Management Seminars, 31 January.

Pollitt, C., Harrison, S., Hunter, D. and Marnoch, G. (1988) 'The reluctant managers: clinicians and budgets in the NHS', *Financial Accountability and Management*, 4(3): 213–34.

Pollitt, C., Harrison, S., Hunter, D. and Marnoch, G. (1991) 'General management in the NHS: the initial impact 1982–88', *Public Administration*, Spring: 61–83.

Pratt, J. (1995) *Practitioners and Practices*, London, BMJ Press.

Press and Journal (1996) February 2: 5.

Pringle, M. (1993) 'Managing change in general practice', in M. Pringle (ed.), *Change and Teamwork in Primary Care*. London, BMJ Press.

Ranade, W. (1994) *A Future for the NHS?: Health Care in the 1990s*, London, Longman.

Roberts, H. (1990) 'Performance and outcome measures in the health service', in M. Cave, M. Kogan and R. Smith (eds), *Output and Performance Measurement in Government*. London, Jessica Kingsley.

Roberts, J. (1993) 'Managing markets', *Journal of Public Health Medicine*, Autumn: 305–10.

Robinson, R. and Le Grand, J. (eds) (1994) *Evaluating the NHS Reforms*. London, Kings Fund Institute.

Roland, M. and Coulter, A. (eds) (1992) *Hospital Referrals*. Oxford, Oxford University Press.

Roland, M. (1992) 'Communication between GPs and Specialists', in M. Roland and A. Coulter, *Hospital Referrals*. Oxford, Oxford University Press.

Rosenthal, M. (1995) *The Incompetent Doctor*. Buckingham, Open University Press.

Rossi, P. and Freeman, H. (1989) *Evaluation: A Systematic Approach*. New York, Sage.

Saltman, R. and von Otter, C. (1992) *Planned Markets and Public Competition: Strategic Reform in Northern European Health Systems*. Buckingham, Open University Press.

Scheiber, G., Poullier, J. and Greenwald, L. (1992) 'US health expenditure performance: an international comparison and data update', *Health Care Financing Review*, 13(4): 1–15.

Scottish Health Services Council (1966) *Administrative Practice in Hospital Boards in Scotland* (Chairman Farquarson-Lang). Edinburgh, HMSO.

Scottish Home and Health Department (1987) Scottish Health Service Planning Council, 'Performance indicators in the Scottish health service', Edinburgh, Scottish Home and Health Department.

Scottish Office Home and Health Department (1990) *Scotland's Health: A Challenge for Us All*. Edinburgh, HMSO.

Scottish Home and Health Department (1994) *Scotland's Health A Challenge To Us All*. Edinburgh, Scottish Home and Health Department.

Sheldon, T. (1994) 'The good guide to guides', *Health Service Journal*, 8 December: 34–5.

Sheridan, T. and Kendall, N. (1992) *Corporate Governance*. London, Pitman.

Shortell, S. (1989) 'New directions in hospital governance', *Hospital and Health Services Administration*, 34(1): 7–23.

Sims, A. and Sims, D. (1993) 'Top teams', *Health Service Journal*, 24 June: 28–9.

Smith, A. and Jacobson, B. (1991) *The Nation's Health: A Strategy for the 1990s*. London, King's Fund Institute.

Social Services Committee (1989) *Resourcing the National Health Service*. London, HMSO.

Southgate, L. (1994) 'Freedom and discipline: clinical practice and the assessment of clinical competence', *British Journal of General Practice*, 44: 87–92.

Soutter, J., Eccles, M. and Newton, J. (1995) *Structure and Function of Partnerships in General Practice: A Pilot Study Centre for Health Services Research*. Newcastle upon Tyne, University of Newcastle.

Spencer, J. (1993) 'Audit in General Practice: where do we go from here?', *Quality in Health Care*, 2(3): 183–8.

Spurgeon, P. (1993a) *The New Face of the NHS*. Harlow, Longman.

Spurgeon, P. (1993b) 'Resource management: a fundamental change in managing health services', in P. Spurgeon, *The New Face of the NHS*. Harlow, Longman.

Stacey, M. (1992) *Regulating British Medicine: The General Medical Council*. Chichester, Wiley.

Stanley, I. and Al-Sheri, A. (1993) 'Re-accreditation: the why, what and how questions', *British Journal of General Practice*, 43: 524–9.

Stewart, R. (1967) *Managers and their Jobs*. London, Macmillan.

Strong, P. and Robinson, J. (1990) *The NHS Under New Management*. Buckingham, Open University Press.

Stuart, J. and Hicks, J. (1993) 'Organization of clinical directorate: Anglo-American experience from laboratory medicine', *The Clinician in Management*, 1(1): 3–5.

Tennison, B. (1992) 'The NHS Review 1988–1991: GPs and contracts for care', in M. Roland and A. Coulter (eds), *Hospital Referrals*. Oxford, Oxford University Press.

Thain, C. (1985) 'The education of the treasury: the medium-term financial strategy', *Public Administration*, 63(3): 261–85.

Thain, C. and Wright, M. (1989) 'The advent of cash planning', *Financial Accountability and Management*, 5(3): 148–62.

The Guardian (1995) 6 June: 4.

Thompson, L. (1992) 'Observations on cost-containment measures and new priorities in the EC by Abel Smith', *Milbank Quarterly*, 70(3): 417–22.

Timmins, N. (1996) *The Five Giants*. London, Fontana.

Vonderemsbe, M. and White, G. (1991) *Operations Management Concepts, Methods and Strategies*. New York, West.

Watson, T. (1994) *In Search of Management*. London, Routledge.

Weiner, J. and Lissovoy, G. (1993) 'A taxonomy for managed care and health insurance plans', *Journal of Health Politics, Policy and Law*, 18(1): 75–103.

Whitby, P. (1994) 'Flights of fancy', *Health Service Journal*, 4 August: 18.

Willcocks, S. (1992) 'The role of clinical director in the NHS: some observations', *Journal of Management in Medicine*, 6(4): 41–6.

Williamson, C. (1992) *Whose Standards?* Buckingham, Open University Press.

Willis, A. (1993) 'General practice – a force for change?', in P. Spurgeon (ed.) (1993a) *The New Face of the NHS*. Harlow, Longman.

Wilson, D. and Rosenfeld, R. (1990) *Managing Organisations*. London, McGraw-Hill.

Index